TRANSFORMATION

Shakespeare's New Theatre

First published in 2011 by RSC Enterprise Ltd
3 Chapel Lane, Stratford-upon-Avon,
Warwickshire, CV37 6BE
www.rsc.org.uk

ISBN: 978-0-9568012-0-3

A catalogue record for this book is available from the British Library.

Designed by The Drawing Room
www.drawingroom.uk.com

Printed and bound in Great Britain by
Hill Shorter Limited, West Bromwich

Printed on GF Smith Colorplan Bright Red/Pristine White duplex (cover), Naturalis Absolute White Smooth (text)

David Ward

TRANSFORMATION
Shakespeare's New Theatre

RSC Enterprise Ltd

Stratford-upon-Avon

Foreword

When I was asked to become Chairman of the RSC in 2004 I didn't fully understand what I would be spending most of my time doing in the ensuing seven years. Neither did anybody else, which is perhaps fortunate, as we might all have chosen an easier, slower and less ambitious path.

The Transformation Project has ended, triumphantly, with a brand new auditorium and the restoration of all that was best in Elisabeth Scott's 1932 theatre, married with the distinctive new elements of the tower, the rooftop restaurant and the colonnade. The 1932 façades have been restored to their former glory, as have the Art Deco interiors; the latter are amongst the finest examples of their period, and it is a joy to see them uncluttered, free from coat racks, ice cream machines and odd carousels. We have sworn a solemn oath to keep them like that. The Swan is linked to the RST for the first time, and there is a magnificent view from the new front of the RST through the reopened carriage entrance of the Swan to Holy Trinity. You can walk along the river from Clopton Bridge past the RST to the church. And it is already clear that we now appear much more welcoming to visitors and residents in Stratford-upon-Avon. Our dressing rooms all have a river view, we have enough ladies' lavatories, and excellent wheelchair access throughout the building.

However, this was not where we began; the starting point for most of us was the debris of expenditure on architects' drawings for a building that was never likely to be built. It took some time to identify the best way forward and to realise that the transformation of the existing RST was not only the most realistic but the best of the available options.

The Project (it deserves its capital P) involved much more than the RST. In the last five years we have:

■ refurbished the Union Club in Chapel Lane

■ built 2,000 square feet of new office accommodation behind the Union Club, and decanted staff out of the RST into these two buildings

■ obtained planning permission for and erected The Courtyard Theatre

■ taken a long lease on and refurbished new rehearsal space in Arden Street

■ taken a long lease on and refurbished new education space on Waterside

■ restarted our nursery school in new premises in Shottery

■ entered into a five-year agreement with the Roundhouse as our London home, and a three-year agreement with Hampstead Theatre for our new work in London

■ refurbished the Arden Hotel in a joint venture with the Eden Hotel Group

That may make the RSC seem like a property company – and there have been moments when bricks and mortar seemed to dominate our lives. So it is worth reminding ourselves that during this period we launched the Spanish Golden Age plays in 2004, the *Complete Works* in 2006-07, the *Histories* cycle in 2006-08 and saw Judi Dench, Ian McKellen, Patrick Stewart, David Warner, Toby Stephens, Vanessa Redgrave, David Tennant, Harriet Walter and Antony Sher strut their stuff with the stars of the future in our ensemble companies. We've toured in the UK, the USA, Spain, Japan, Australia and New Zealand, launched the successful Stand Up For Shakespeare campaign and reinvigorated our work with schools.

Good buildings are important – but they can only enhance, not guarantee, good performances. Our transformed RST is, we believe, one of the finest stages for Shakespeare's plays anywhere in the world. We have kept the ghosts; you can walk on the original boards of the old RST stage just outside the auditorium, and Sir Ian Richardson's ashes are buried underneath the front row of the stalls. But it is the performances still to come from successive generations of RSC actors, directors, designers and musicians that will set the stamp of greatness on the RST.

John Masefield, in his poem written for the opening of the theatre in 1932, wrote of:

The acted passion, beautiful and swift,
The spirit leaping out of flesh and bone

We can look forward with confidence and excitement to seeing that passion, that spirit, leaping out from the stage of our transformed RST.

None of this could have been achieved without a prodigious amount of dedication and hard work by the staff of the RSC, our Project Committees and Design Groups, our architects, engineers, project managers, theatre consultants and acousticians. And the great generosity of our patrons, foremost amongst whom are Arts Council England, Advantage West Midlands, David and Susie Sainsbury and The Gatsby Charitable Foundation, the Weston family and many others. I salute and thank them.

Sir Christopher Bland, *Chairman*

01.

Ten days before Midsummer's Day in 2006, actor Richard Cordery walked on to the thrust stage of the Royal Shakespeare Company's new Courtyard Theatre in Stratford-upon-Avon, pointed to a woman in the front row and said:

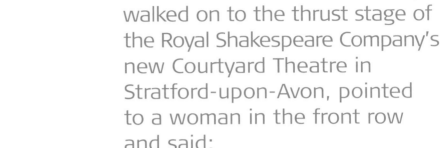

The Courtyard Theatre's first audience applauds the theatre rehearsal

The audience begins to assemble for the theatre rehearsal

'It's hard to imagine, madam, but 11 months ago I parked my car exactly where you are sitting.'

The Courtyard was created in a rush in a rectangular shed made from the same rusty steel that the sculptor Antony Gormley had used for his Angel of the North. The theatre, built on a car park, would serve as the RSC's temporary home during the Transformation project, a £112.8 million scheme to create The Courtyard, new offices, new rehearsal rooms and an entirely new auditorium within the walls (or what was left of them) of the Royal Shakespeare Theatre. The scheme was intended to reconstruct both the building and the reputation of the Company, which had been through some troubled times.

The first Courtyard audience, made up of builders, contractors, the people of Stratford, RSC staff and actors, had filed in to see the new rich, red auditorium for what was billed as a 'theatre rehearsal'. The Rev Martin Gorick,

01

vicar of Holy Trinity, Stratford, and the RSC's Honorary Chaplain, had already had a preview. He had walked alone on to the stage, gazed about and cried: 'This would make a lovely church.'

Samuel West spoke the first lines of Shakespeare in the new theatre when he read from the opening speech of the Chorus in *Henry V* ('O, for a muse of fire, that would ascend / The brightest heaven of invention . . .'). The speech refers to a theatre as a wooden O rather than a steel box, but no one quibbled.

Cordery, dapper in a dinner suit, introduced a variety of brief performances: Kieran Hill sang an aria from Puccini's *Turandot*; Harriet Walter played Gertrude in a send-up of *Hamlet* by Margaret Atwood (and all but stole the show); the young bloods of Verona performed the fight scene from *Romeo and Juliet*; and Tim Pigott-Smith spoke Prospero's famous lines whose references to theatrical impermanence seemed perfect for a theatre that would be here today and gone a few tomorrows hence:

The cloud-capped towers, the gorgeous palaces,
The solemn temples, the great globe itself,
Yea, all which it inherit, shall dissolve,
And, like this insubstantial pageant faded,
Leave not a rack behind.

High up in the theatre, Andy Hayles, Managing Director of Charcoalblue, the theatre consultants who had worked

Richard Cordery on stage during the theatre rehearsal

'This would make a lovely church . . .' The audience waits for the theatre rehearsal to begin

on the auditorium as part of the RSC team, had returned to his old job (for one night only) as a follow spot operator: his shins – though not his head or torso – are clearly visible in one of the publicity photographs taken that night. 'The atmosphere was electric, amazing. We couldn't believe we had got away with it and how good it was. It was a big night, a big moment for us.'

Others involved in the Transformation project were similarly excited. 'The builders' night was just fantastic,' said Susie Sainsbury, Deputy Chair of the RSC, who was greatly relieved by the prospect of success after the turmoil of the previous few years. 'In deciding to build The Courtyard, we had done something very brave and very bold; we had gone for it wholeheartedly and it had been an extremely cheery and benign process. We had shown everyone that we could deliver what we said we were going to deliver.'

'It was a very exciting building to walk into. That first night, with all those people in the auditorium, we thought, "This theatre is real, this is what we wanted. It has an excitement about it, a connection with the other people in the audience." It was quite extraordinary.'

'Evenings like that are always complicated because you are exhausted and have a heightened sense of emotion,' added Vikki Heywood, the RSC's Executive Director. 'You are very aware that there is an enormous group of people around you who are absolutely exhausted too. But there was a sense that we were going to turn this into a space and that it was going to work.'

Sir Christopher Bland, Chairman of the RSC, felt 'utter rapture. It was terrific.' Michael Boyd, the RSC's Artistic Director, walked on to the stage and declared with impressive certainty: 'This is a meeting place between audience and actors where we can make some kind of fragile consensus together.' That night and the first year of performances that followed strengthened his conviction that his bold decision to commit the RSC to a thrust stage was the right one.

On 7 July 2006, a month after the builders' night, the first paying audience packed The Courtyard for its first Shakespeare play. Boyd's production of *Henry VI, Part I* went on without a dress rehearsal; time had run out as cast and crew familiarised themselves with the new stage – and actors learned to descend from the roof via ropes and ladders – as Boyd showed off what his new space could do.

Nine months later, in a performance of *Coriolanus* on 31 March 2007, a blood-spattered William Houston, playing the flawed Roman hero, became the last actor to die on the proscenium arch stage of the 1932 Royal Shakespeare Theatre. The last word of the last play on that stage was Aufidius' 'Assist'. 'The rest is silence' might have been a better way to end 75 years of theatre history. But Aufidius' final speech had one concession to the occasion: 'I am struck with sorrow,' a sentiment that caught the mood of many in the auditorium that night.

This marked the end of Boyd's great *Complete Works* cycle – a festival season in which each of Shakespeare's 37 plays was staged in Stratford in a single year – and was, for both actors and audience, a night full of nostalgia for what had been and anticipation of what was to come: for many the pain of saying goodbye to the Royal Shakespeare Theatre in its old form had been eased by the success of The Courtyard. They had glimpsed a vision of the RST's future and it appeared to be working.

William Houston as Coriolanus, the final production on the proscenium arch stage of the RST

01.

Many present at that *Coriolanus* had memories of school trips to Stratford. They had entered the theatre not through its elegant foyer but through the ignominious side door and had then climbed up grim concrete steps to the balcony, with its uncomfortable seats, little red binoculars and distant view of the stage. 'It was like being a spectator at someone else's party,' said one.

The presence of David Warner in the audience reminded many of his 1965 *Hamlet*. But Edward Timms' memories reached back much further. Timms, then approaching his 93rd birthday, watched *Coriolanus* from a seat in row M in the stalls. He had seen the old Victorian Shakespeare Memorial Theatre burn down in 1926 and saw the first production in Elisabeth Scott's new building shortly after it opened in 1932. He had been a regular ever since and seen them all: Laurence Olivier, Vivien Leigh, Paul Scofield, John Gielgud, Peggy Ashcroft.

His favourite Lear was Donald Sinden. 'I feel very sad that this theatre is going because it has given me many happy memories,' he said. 'But I'm sure people will take to the new building. It will be a renewed challenge. The new auditorium will be more intimate for audiences and the proscenium here has always been a barrier between actor and audience.'

Gregory Doran, the RSC's Chief Associate Director, director of *Coriolanus* and the voice of the recording that for some years had urged RST patrons to take their seats when the performance was about to begin, suggested, in a phrase that came to haunt the whole Transformation project, that ghosts were locked inside walls soon to be battered into rubble by demolition teams. Everyone in the audience was then urged by Michael Boyd to rise from their seats and give a standing ovation to the theatre and all who had played in it. And so they did.

That *Coriolanus* performance was only the first in a three-

night run of farewells. There was another emotional goodbye at the RSC Open Day a couple of weeks later when the RSC band played incidental music from productions ranging from Raymond Leppard's music for Sir Peter Hall's 1959 production of *A Midsummer Night's Dream* (with novelist Margaret Drabble as a fairy) to Paul Englishby's score for *Merry Wives – The Musical* (2006). The concert ended with a massed chorus singing Hand In Hand from Guy Woolfenden's score for Sir Trevor Nunn's 1976 *The Comedy of Errors*.

The final performance in the auditorium was a private farewell attended by past and present Company members and staff. 'We wanted a ceremony, a moment when we put the theatre to sleep. The Company needed that,' said Heywood. 'I was petrified, overburdened with the responsibility of knowing that I had to honour the emotion that was in that room at that moment.'

'I cried. We all did,' said Sainsbury. 'Half of the greatest actors of my lifetime were holding hands with tears pouring down their faces.'

'That night made it very clear how important it had been in the theatrical lives of everyone who came on stage and told good stories,' added Bland. 'It was an extraordinary range of people.'

Among them was Sir Ian McKellen, who had played Romeo, Leontes and Macbeth at the RST. 'I think a lot of people who were crying that night, including those who had worked there a lot more than I had, were thinking "Is this a wake? Is it a celebration? Are we delighted the theatre is going?" Everyone on the stage had been in performances that in their minds were unforgettable and yet they were at an event at which the destruction of the building was being marked. Whether celebrated is the word, I don't know. People were in two minds and I was too.'

A standing ovation for the RST, 31 March 2007

Doran put together a programme that featured many great names: Dame Judi Dench spoke one of Titania's speeches and, as Sainsbury put it, 'became 25 again'. Elizabeth Spriggs, an RSC stalwart in the 1960s and 70s, spoke Paulina's words from the end of *The Winter's Tale* and Tony Church, a founder member of the Company, declaimed the John of Gaunt speech from *Richard II*.

Church, by then quite frail, had feared he would not remember his lines and so was fed them by his son. 'At the end, Tony put out his hand to tell his son to stop and intoned "This blessed plot, this earth, this realm, this England",' said Doran. 'It was a magnificent moment. He was passing his talent on, having become too frail to practise it himself.'

Sir Ian McKellen, Dame Judi Dench and Maureen Beattie at the private farewell to the RST

(Church had a special reason to remember the stage on which he made his RSC debut in *The Two Gentlemen of Verona* in 1960. He had one line and planned to deliver it languidly while leaning on his sword. 'My sword disappeared down a crack between the floor and the revolving stage and I fell flat on my arse on my first utterance on the stage in that theatre.')

Michael Boyd addresses the audience on the last night of *Coriolanus*

Doran also brought together five RSC Hamlets: Toby Stephens (then the most recent) began 'To be or not to be' and the speech was completed by Samuel West, Mark Rylance, Michael Pennington and David Warner.

'That night there was a wonderful gathering of an extraordinary concentration of leading actors in quiet community on that stage,' said Boyd. 'They had a modest eloquence and humility about them and if you hadn't felt emotional about the theatre before, you certainly would then.'

At the last night of *Coriolanus*, Boyd had seemed, for once, a little lost for words, as if overtaken by unexpectedly strong emotions. 'We have been wandering around a bit like lost things today,' he told the people in the purple seats before him. Then he ambled over to thump the bare, exposed brickwork at the side of the stage. 'Whatever happens, these walls, this proscenium stays. This is a stage from which so many extraordinary talents have given their heart and soul.'

The first truth was that the proscenium had to stay: it was part of the fly tower and any attempt to remove that would have reduced the theatre to ruins because it was holding the building up. The second truth was that while Boyd understood utterly the feelings of many of those in the theatre that night, he was determined to get on with a job that had to be done. He had entertained no sentimental thoughts of his own as he smacked that wall. 'I felt, "Thank God, this is all coming down",' he said. 'I felt no guilt. Of course it's a big thing and it has to be done with tact and with love. But the RSC is too important and the stakes too high to just have a nice warm bath in the past. It's not possible.'

The Avon façade of the 1932
Shakespeare Memorial Theatre

02

Actors and directors began complaining about Elisabeth Scott's Shakespeare Memorial Theatre (as the Royal Shakespeare Theatre was then called) almost as soon as it opened in 1932 with a matinée performance of *Henry IV, Part I.*

Scott herself was sure she had balanced the needs of drama and architecture and said (when appointed in 1927 at the age of 29): 'I belong to the Modernist school of architects. By that I mean I believe the function of the building to be the most important thing to be considered. In terms of theatre, this means that acoustics and sightlines must come first. At the same time, I have taken full advantage of the exceptionally beautiful site on the banks of the Avon.'

Sir Archibald Flower, Chairman of the theatre's governors, had already proclaimed that

'nothing but the best is good enough for Shakespeare'.

Elisabeth Scott, architect

A report on the new theatre in *Architect and Building News* in April 1932 suggested in somewhat tortuous prose that the architectural world was impressed: 'While it is as efficient a vehicle for the presentation of plays as the resources of modern theatre design and construction can make it, as a work of architecture it reveals that no less thought and time have been expended on small details than on greater matters, a thing all too rare in modern building.'

02

Those details included a stage curtain of artificial silk velvet with claret and black central panels radiating sideways and upwards through lighter shades to red, grey, rich yellows and white; decorative woodwork that covered the walls of the dress circle, with horizontal veneers of Australian walnut and inlays of ebony and rosewood; and finger plates on the rear doors formed from aluminium alloy shaped into the masks of comedy and tragedy.

The interior may have been beautiful but the theatre's limitations soon became clear: despite Scott's best intentions, neither the acoustics nor the sightlines were that good. Nor was the building, to quote again one of the clumsiest and most utilitarian descriptions of a theatre, 'an efficient vehicle for the presentation of plays'. In design and construction the balance had tipped in favour of architecture rather than drama, possibly because no theatre professional had been permanently available to keep watch while building was in progress.

Forty years later, Iain Mackintosh, founder of theatre consultants Theatre Projects, analysed what had gone wrong with the Memorial Theatre: 'The lesson of Stratford is twofold: firstly, that despite the fact that the client did say clearly what he wanted, he did not get it, although he thought all was well until the opening night; secondly, that the architect thought she had created what she had not: a focused, intimate theatre.

'The theatre profession, when roused, is more vociferous than the architectural profession and the nation accepted the theatrical view: it was all the fault of the architect. It is clear that there had been a breakdown in communications between the two professions.'

The theatre had fundamental problems. For a start, the only through route from the auditorium to backstage areas was across the stage. Dressing rooms were poky

Details from the 1932 theatre – and a poky dressing room

and inadequate and there were only two small offices for administrative staff.

William Bridges-Adams, Director of the annual Shakespeare Festival, had asked for a horseshoe-shaped auditorium but was presented with the fan shape then common in new cinemas being built across the country. He also asked for, and got, a proscenium arch but ended up with a deep forestage (with orchestra pit) that became an almost unbridgeable gulf between actors and audience.

If that was a gulf, there was a mighty chasm between the stage and the remote balcony, which had not been in Scott's original design.

Hard-up theatregoers (most of them school students) found themselves far removed from the stage: from here, the face of Macbeth or Viola was merely a blur and only those with hyperopia might catch a glimpse of Gloucester's gouged-out eye.

Sir Archibald Flower, a member of the Stratford brewing dynasty and nephew of Charles Edward Flower, whose donation of land and funds had helped create the original Shakespeare Memorial Theatre in 1879, was not one to be challenged by theatre people. He kept Bridges-Adams in his place, which was backstage. In an interview recorded just before her death at the age of 96 in 2009, Lady Hersey Flower, wife of Sir Archibald's son Fordham, said: 'My father-in-law said Bridges' authority was from the fire curtain backwards – but nothing in front. The auditorium was nothing to do with Bridges and [Sir Archibald] would accept no thoughts or criticism or advice on it.

'My father-in-law thought that the one thing that mattered was that people should hear the words. He was right. But he also thought that there should be absolutely nothing to distract the human eye from the hole in the wall that gives you the words. So the Memorial Theatre was exactly like a cinema. All the people who played in it and directed in it would grumble to my husband about the unresponsiveness of the audience, that they were so distant from the audience and that there was nothing but bare walls for their jokes to echo from. They felt it was dead. My husband always took the side of the directors and actors who would like a different auditorium. But they weren't going to get it.'

A mighty chasm: a view from the stage to the back of the Memorial Theatre

Bridges-Adams, who was later to describe the building as 'the theatre, of all theatres, in England in which it is hardest to make an audience laugh or cry', left Stratford a disappointed man. Balliol Holloway, a long-serving Memorial Theatre actor, led the Shakespeare Festival company in the 1934 season and soon found plenty to complain about: 'The acres of blank walls between the proscenium arch and the ends of the circles, coupled with the immense distance between the lower edge of the stage proper and the front row of the stalls, destroys completely all contact between actors and audience.'

It was, he added, 'like trying to act from Calais to the cliffs of Dover',

a phrase borrowed more than 70 years later by Sir Christopher Bland, Chairman of the RSC, when he launched the design for the transformed RST to the media in London. 'It was fine as an auditorium if you had a good seat,' Bland said later. 'But I sat in the back at the top and knew that you could neither see nor hear in the cheapest seats and that's where a lot of people started their first, and no doubt in some cases their last, experiences of Shakespeare.'

In 1939, theatre director Norman Marshall said the gulf between stage and auditorium would be serious enough in any theatre 'but is doubly so in a theatre built for the plays of Shakespeare, which were written for a platform stage with no proscenium and no barrier of any sort between actor and audience.'

Later artistic directors and managers, frustrated by perceived limitations and desperate to make audiences giggle or sob more readily, came up with schemes to modify the stage, auditorium and other parts of the building. Extensions provided a café, a green room, extra dressing rooms, seats in side balconies, plus much-needed extra toilets. (There were never enough: most women in the audience had to choose between an interval drink or the queue for the ladies'.)

In 1944, the orchestra pit was covered by a floor level with the stage. Six years later, Sir Anthony Quayle, appointed by Sir Fordham Flower to run the annual festival, was horrified by what he found. In his memoir *A Time to Speak* (1990), he did not mince his words:

'The building was of a hideousness that nobody who had not sat in it could possibly appreciate. It was built like a cinema, a long shoe-box of a place. The walls were lined with big panels of French-polished wood. These panels were not only garish to look at but light bounced off them during the action of the play. The dress circle was set so far back that you were almost sitting outside the theatre. It was a monstrosity. One of the first jobs that I was obliged to do was to pull the dress circle nearer to the stage, thrust two wings out on either side so that the dress circle audience was linked visually and physically with the action, and tear down the dreadful strips of shiny veneer.'

When appointed Managing Director (by Sir Fordham Flower) in 1958, Sir Peter Hall told the *Coventry Evening Telegraph* that he would like to demolish the building (which, with the founding of the Royal Shakespeare Company in 1961, became known as the Royal Shakespeare Theatre). But the governors failed to call in the wreckers so when he took up the job a year later he set about modifying the auditorium, working with stage designer Henry Bardon to reconfigure the problematic forestage into a hexagon with the front rows of the stalls grouped around it. In an article about Hall's changes, the critic Penelope Gilliatt said the audience 'would have a sense of sitting *around* the stage, instead of facing it balefully through a proscenium arch.'

Troilus and Cressida on the hexagonal front stage introduced by Sir Peter Hall

'It was an attempt to relate the stage much more intimately to the auditorium and vice versa,' said Hall 50 years later. 'We were trying to get a feeling that actors and audience inhabited the same room rather than confronting each other. It worked marginally. It didn't work because it had the same problems as Anthony Quayle had had. The circle came round and approached the stage on each side, which was a help. But I certainly had a feeling at the very beginning that the people in the balcony were having a very different experience from the people in the stalls.

'The hexagon remained in place throughout my time in one form or another. We kept pushing a bit here and another bit there, extending and cutting back. It was like some kind of growth that had to be looked after. But we never got it right and the reason we never got it right was because you couldn't get it right. I think it was a very handsome Art Deco building but it had very little to do with play-acting. It was a complete expression of the time and we kept on struggling with it.'

Hall and Sean Kenny (designer of the famous sets for the original production of Lionel Bart's *Oliver!*) had considered a more radical scheme in 1961, the year Hall launched the Royal Shakespeare Company. Kenny said at the time: 'We would like to replace the old stage and auditorium with an open amphitheatre stage, with the audience on three sides and a flying grid over the forestage. We feel this type of stage is essential if Shakespeare is to be produced properly. It would make the plays live again – they've been boxed up for too long.'

By 1973, the RST had acquired side balconies and slips that helped create a rather strait-laced version of the horseshoe Bridges-Adams had sought. But by then Bridges-Adams (known as Unabridges-Adams because of his liking for uncut performances of Shakespeare plays) had been dead for eight years. In 1976, during

Sir Trevor Nunn's tenure as Artistic Director, the side galleries were extended through the proscenium and round the back of the stage to create a link between actors and audience. Some members of the public sat in those on-stage galleries during performances and enjoyed a unique back-view of Shakespeare's plays.

'That was a very congenial place and I loved doing Romeo there and people loved sitting on the stage close to the action. It made one long even more for a theatre that wasn't a proscenium theatre,' said Sir Ian McKellen. 'The theatre was large. It tested the voice but I have never really heard anybody who saw plays complaining about what they saw. It was the people doing the plays who felt they had the problem.'

Adrian Noble, Michael Boyd's predecessor, first directed in the RST in 1982 and remembers an annual struggle – mostly creative – between directors and the space. 'A major issue was the volume of air and the distance between the actor and the people in the poorest seats. A very large number of seats were up in the balcony and those people were, without question, disadvantaged. All the subsequent revisits of the directors during the 1980s and 1990s were in some way variations upon that theme.'

Modifications included projecting the forestage into the audience as a semicircle and adding runways down the aisles in the stalls to allow actors to sprint through the audience and straight on to the stage. In 1986-7, bench seats were placed on either side of the forestage and in 1988 two banks of seats were built to drop from either side of the dress circle to the stage – but the view of the action of many people sitting in the side stalls was greatly obscured (they suffered particularly badly in Sir Nicholas Hytner's production of The Tempest) and the seats were soon removed.

The set for *Hamlet* in 2001, with new forestage and runway down an aisle

Romeo and Juliet in 1976, with on-stage galleries; and Sir Ian McKellen as Romeo

In 2001, Noble revealed a £100,000 short-term revamp of the auditorium that he had worked on with designer Alison Chitty, who had built a forestage across the entire 17-metre width of the auditorium to give an outer and an inner stage and bring the actors closer to the circle and the balcony. 'The problem is that the gods are totally cut off from the experience of the theatre,' said Chitty in a later interview. 'I'm conscious that there are a lot of young people there and they are miles away, physically and psychologically. That's a tough one . . . We were anxious first of all to try to make it better for kids up on the top deck, at the same time managing the whole relationship between the audience and the stage.'

Chitty had wanted to go much further and create what sounded like a version of Sean Kenny's arena. 'Our first plan was to do away with the circle and stalls and just bring the seats down in one sweep to the stage floor,' she said. 'It looked fantastic but it was impossibly expensive.'

The Chitty project was the last of the many attempts to make the RST work better. Noble and Michael Boyd would separately decide that no more could be done and that the tinkerings had to be replaced by more radical solutions: one would propose that the building should be flattened; the other that a new auditorium should be created within it.

03

As an orchestra rehearsed Tchaikovsky's 1812 Overture in a hall next door, the RSC's Foundation Board met at the Barbican in London in 1995 to discuss the creation of an endowment fund aimed at protecting the Company in case of revenue funding problems under present or future governments.

When Adrian Noble, the Company's Artistic Director and Chief Executive, was asked about his hopes and plans for the future, he stunned the Board's members by saying that

he wasn't interested in an endowment fund; what he wanted was a new theatre.

View from across the river showing the former restaurant and café

An aerial view of the RST before Transformation

And so Noble announced an ambition that turned into a plan that came to nothing and led to his decision to leave a company he had joined as a director in 1980. But that day at the Barbican, as Tchaikovsky's cannons boomed and triumphant bells rang out, Susie Sainsbury and her Foundation Board colleagues began to think favourably of Noble's idea. They all agreed that a capital campaign was infinitely sexier and much easier to raise money for than an endowment fund, and that maybe the endowment should come on the back of or after a new theatre.

In August 1998, *The Independent* broke the story of Noble's wish to demolish the 1932 theatre and Noble himself set out his case in the paper a few days later, explaining that over the years the RST had been 'cudgelled, reshaped and revamped' with only limited success. The conclusion was clear: the Royal Shakespeare Theatre would have to come down and be replaced by a new adaptable auditorium to be used for both thrust stage and proscenium productions.

The RSC had appointed the young Dutch architect Erick van Egeraat, now best known in Britain for his Middlesbrough Institute of Modern Art, to start preliminary work in 1997. Van Egeraat came over from Holland and gave what Sainsbury described as an 'absolutely dazzling' presentation that analysed the RST's problems and the Company's position in Stratford and the world. 'It was a remarkable *tour de force* and we were all totally smitten by this young European architect,' she said. 'We went to Holland to see some of the things he had done and were very impressed. He appeared to understand what he could and couldn't do. He was charismatic, charming and talented.'

Iain Mackintosh from theatre design specialists Theatre Projects was brought in as theatre consultant and carried out an in-depth study of the existing building and its history. The RSC also applied to Arts Council England for a National Lottery grant towards a scheme then estimated to cost £100 million. After an investigation of the RSC, the Council earmarked £50 million in 1999 but said the funds would not be released until the Company had completed an internal restructuring. In 2000, the Council handed over £714,000 towards a £3.3 million feasibility study led by van Egeraat, who formally signed a contract the same year.

The Barbican, former London home of the RSC

How the *Stratford-upon-Avon Herald* reported Erick van Egeraat's scheme

But the Board faced worrying uncertainties and snags. For a start, English Heritage was adamantly opposed to the destruction of the theatre, which, as obstacles go, was a pretty big one. Nor could the kind of adaptable theatre Noble wanted be constructed within the existing RST, even if English Heritage allowed it to be knocked about.

Some Board members wandered the world to look at flexible theatres with both proscenium and thrust stages while others explored 15 other potential construction sites in Stratford, including the Arden Hotel (owned by the RSC but at the time leased to Thistle Hotels), the Bancroft Gardens by the Avon, a boatyard north of Clopton Bridge, the old cattle market on Alcester Road and the Bell Court shopping centre in the heart of the town (convenient for shopping in Debenhams).

In May 2001 the RSC announced, under the curious headline 'A new deal with artists and audiences', what became known as Project Fleet, a plan to make the Company 'more agile, more flexible and less institutional'. It said little about a new theatre for Stratford but a great deal about Noble's plans for the future. The Company would pull out of the Barbican, which had been its London home since 1982; abandon the long-term ensemble system that could bind an actor to the RSC for up to two years in favour of short contracts designed to appeal to actors with parallel careers in film and television; and create in Stratford an academy in which to train the next generation of classical actors.

The day after the announcement, Michael Boyd, then an Associate Director, told *The Guardian* that the RSC was in danger of crumbling under the weight of its traditions.

He supported plans to shake up the contract system with actors, a position he was to develop shortly after.

There was a price to pay for this mould-breaking: most of the 80 jobs at the Barbican would go, along with another 50 or 60 in Stratford. There was an initial flurry of headlines over the plan to quit the London base but media coverage was broadly positive, with Michael Billington in *The Guardian* writing of a 'radical restructuring born of pragmatic necessity'.

But he added a cautionary note:

'In a world of flash and dazzle, isn't there still something radical and moving about the notion of a permanent company bound together by life values as well as art?'

When, a few days later, Benedict Nightingale, theatre critic of *The Times*, expressed similar reservations, Noble responded with a detailed defence of his plan in the same paper. Within weeks the critical noise was growing louder. 'Is Adrian Noble steering the RSC towards disaster?' bellowed *The Sunday Times* in July.

Undaunted, Noble pressed on. By the summer of 2001, the results of the feasibility study into what was to be done about the theatres in Stratford were ready to be sent to Arts Council England and on 18 August the RSC issued a press release that began: 'The Royal Shakespeare Company is set to create a new waterfront theatre village, redeveloping its historic home in Stratford.' The release went on to explain that the Company was going to 'rebuild a landmark modern Shakespeare playhouse on the riverside site of the current Royal Shakespeare Theatre'. (The word 'demolition' appeared nowhere in the release.) The RSC would also build a permanent new theatre to replace the RST, create a flexible space with

between 250 and 600 seats, and would set up the promised academy for young actors.

The formal announcement intensified the fuss that had already been brewing in the media, among RSC staff and especially in Stratford: at that time the RSC was worth £32 million a year to the local economy and owners of shops, restaurants and guest houses wanted to be sure that the cash would continue to roll in. But that word 'village', used apparently in all innocence, turned out to be a disaster; the kind of disaster that will find its way into public relations training manuals. It was nothing less than a Gerald Ratner 'crap' moment. Noble was quite clear what the word meant in this context but soon came to realise that the world beyond the banks of the Avon had chosen to interpret it in a completely different way.

The 18 August press release was accompanied by Noble's own account (which did include the word 'demolition') of why redevelopment had to happen. The Royal Shakespeare Theatre was 'dysfunctional', a building 'where some have a much better experience than others, making it an extremely undemocratic theatre'.

There was no denying Noble's enthusiasm for and commitment to his scheme. The morning after details had been announced, a *Guardian* leader headlined 'A stage for all the world' added its criticisms of the RST and proclaimed that seeing a play there all too often had a feeling of anticlimax about it. 'The Royal Shakespeare Company's plan to demolish its theatre in Stratford is . . . great news. The thought of it being replaced by an appropriate and handsome theatre building, and for the theatre to be the working centrepiece of a really top-class set of Shakespearean visitor attractions, is a thrilling national opportunity.'

Any euphoria this endorsement produced was short-lived. The day the enthusiastic leader appeared in *The Guardian*,

The Independent reported growing opposition: the Twentieth Century Society was 'very alarmed' about the demolition plan; an English Heritage spokesman said no proposal to tear down the theatre had been submitted. 'That would be a severe test for us,' he added ominously. It got worse: three weeks after Noble issued his press release, Terry Hands, former Artistic Director of the RSC and the man who had groomed Noble for the top job, resigned as the Company's Advisory Director, saying he could not see how the plans could be artistically or financially viable.

A couple of weeks later, RSC backstage staff at the Barbican voted to strike over redundancy plans and *The Independent* analysed the Company's problems under the headline 'A tragicomedy of our times', with a suggestion that RSC now stood for Rancour, Subterfuge, Calamity. The story also pointed out that Noble was about to take a three-month paid sabbatical from the RSC to direct a 'wholly commercial' production of *Chitty Chitty Bang Bang* in London.

Meanwhile, 'village' had become a dirty word. In his press release on 18 August, Noble had suggested what the concept meant to him. 'Our newly-built theatres will be open 16 hours a day and they will become prime destinations for Stratford residents, audiences and tourists. For the first time people will be able to pass through our spaces, perhaps enjoying an exhibition or a concert or just sitting and enjoying the river. Stratford and the RSC will then be ready to become a true magnet for artists and audiences from all over the world.'

The implication was that the Company wanted to open up the RSC's site, to bring in people to see and enjoy the work and environment of a national company supported by their taxes even if they were not interested in experiencing a performance.

STRATFORD TO GET TWO NEW THEATRES

From the *Herald's* four-page wrap-around

The map of the theatre village

With the help of the RSC, the *Stratford-upon-Avon Herald* had run a four-page comprehensive wrap-around about the announcement on 18 October. In it, the village concept was more closely defined: 'The proposed theatre village will offer a range of accessible experiences, from the full impact of RSC performances, through straightforward fun and general interest for all ages – perhaps stage make-up, a prop-making demonstration, shopping or the backstage tour – to a study of a text or an acting masterclass for the serious student. The experience should be high quality but not always high-minded, sometimes offering the profound experience of theatre, and sometimes simple enjoyment such as a good meal, the river and gardens, or good busking.'

These aims seem at worst unobjectionable and at best inspirational, a natural extension of the plan to make the new RST a more democratic space than the old one. A serious playgoer might well enjoy a little textual study of *Hamlet* before seeing a performance; a teenager lured into a fight workshop might be tempted to see Agincourt re-enacted in *Henry V*. But the concept of the open-to-all Shakespeare village never caught on because, in the media and in the mind of the public, it morphed into something completely different: the RSC was going to

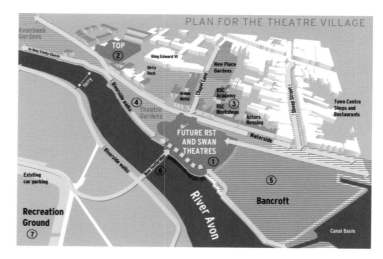

open a Shakespeare theme park. Disney, the word went round, is coming to the Avon. Desdemona would ride a rollercoaster before expiring under Othello's pillow.

Chris Towner, editor of the *Herald*, suggests why the morphing happened: as the RSC announced its Shakespeare village, a Stratford resident and sometime film producer announced his Shakespeare World. Kris Kliszewicz, Chief Executive of Will Power Holdings, said he wanted to build in or near Stratford an authentic recreation of the Tudor market town that had nurtured the world's greatest playwright. There would be actors in costume, Tudor food and contemporary pastimes (but no roller-coasters). The cost of all this was £100 million – exactly the price tag the RSC had put on its reconstruction and Shakespeare village scheme. The confusion was under-standable. 'At the time Noble was promoting a theatre village, you had Kliszewicz promoting his scheme for a Shakespeare theme park,' said Towner. 'There were two separate plans but in the mind of the public they merged.'

The Observer later ran a story that described the Shakespeare village and Shakespeare World and clearly defined the origins of both. But the headline probably helped muddy the murky waters still further:

'All the world's a stage or a theme park'.

In February 2002, the RSC issued a press release that suggested that the plan to demolish the RST was not as cut and dried as the previous autumn's announcement had suggested. Noble's plans for the RST and his Company were running into crisis. The bad headlines kept coming. In March, Michael Billington asked in *The Guardian*: 'Is something rotten in the state of Stratford?' Demolishing the RST could prove to be 'a costly folly'; quitting the Barbican was 'a crass mistake'. Dominic Cavendish's *Daily Telegraph* account of the RSC's troubles on 30 March was headed by a quote from *A Midsummer Night's Dream*: 'Lord, what fools these mortals be!'; *The Observer's* analysis the next day concentrated on Noble and asked: 'Is the RSC safe in his hands?'.

John Peter in *The Sunday Times* was later to suggest that 'some thought [Noble] had confused his calling with that of his father, an undertaker . . . Morale, scribes recorded, was as low as a strumpet's neckline'.

By 24 April 2002, the day after Shakespeare's birthday and eight days after *Chitty Chitty Bang Bang* had opened to rave reviews at the London Palladium, Noble had had enough: he resigned. An RSC statement said he was going to 'seek new artistic challenges'.

'It is an open question whether Adrian had been looking for an escape route for a long time,' said Sainsbury. 'He was having a very difficult time because he was being assailed on all sides both in critical terms and in terms of what he was accused of doing in Stratford. I think he was just utterly miserable.' Writing in *The Guardian*, Michael Billington commented: '[Noble] is a decent man and a very good director who has become the victim of his political naivety. He has tried to revolutionise an institution that needed only gradualist reform.'

Adrian Noble, the RSC's former Artistic Director, found that the months leading up to his resignation were 'a terrible, terrible time'

and remembers the exact moment when he decided to quit: it followed a tough interview with Jeremy Paxman on *Newsnight* on 28 March 2002 during final rehearsals for his London production of *Chitty Chitty Bang Bang*. Newspapers at that time were predicting that the coming RSC season was going to be a disaster. 'I realised that the die had been cast,' he said. 'I couldn't even win on the artistic front of good shows. I couldn't win these battles and had become part of the problem.'

Asked if he was bitter about the way his long service with the RSC ended, he said: 'I don't know. I hope not because I have had a very nice time since I left. But I couldn't win and that's a very frustrating position to be in. It is sometimes galling when I look at the things that have happened subsequently that could have happened only because of the structural changes that I made. There doesn't seem to be any credit passed back.

'But I suppose that's the way of the world.'

Noble's determination to seek a new theatre for Stratford derived from a conviction that nothing more could be done to improve the RST and a realisation that the National Lottery could at last provide the kind of big money a grand design would need. 'The idea of a new theatre never really entered anybody's thinking until the Lottery came along because the sums of money were far too big.

The Swan Theatre

The interior of the Swan, 1986

04

'We always believed we would be incrementally trying to improve the auditorium. But we all knew, because we had spent what seemed like months of our lives working on it, that the RST as it stood had certain structural problems that were insurmountable.'

Two interiors: the Swan (left) and old RST (right)

'If you dropped the end of your lines in the main house, you could not be heard at the back. The RST could be a very cruel space and I've been round to dressing rooms after the first preview to find actors new to the RSC weeping.'

There were also significant artistic problems: experienced actors loved the Swan and were increasingly reluctant to return to the RST; younger actors felt ill at ease in the wide-open spaces of the 1932 theatre.

'The Swan is an unusually sympathetic space. There is a harmony between capacity and volume and the size of the stage is correct.

'During the 1980s and 1990s, some younger actors became less equipped to deal with the main stage because their grounding in verse speaking was less thorough than that of actors who came through earlier. That's partly because the repertory system wasn't there any more, partly because young directors were less interested in verse than when I was their age.

'To make the RST effective as a space, you had to work the language.

The kind of new theatre Noble had in mind was one in which actors would be surrounded by the audience on three sides, a plan that bore some similarity to what was created first at The Courtyard and then at the new RST. But there was a significant difference, one that triggered a crisis and led ultimately to Noble's departure. The RST, like The Courtyard before it, is now a thrust stage, and only thrust stage, theatre. Noble wanted flexibility, a theatre that could present plays in both proscenium arch and thrust stage configurations (although the thrust stage in his preferred scheme would have been only half as deep as that in The Courtyard).

'I did not feel that I could impose on every director and artistic director who came after me the necessity of directing everything on a thrust stage at the RSC. I could not say to a director, "You can never direct behind a proscenium arch inside one of our home theatres ever again".'

Noble consulted engineers who told him that precious little could be done to achieve the kind of theatre he

wanted within the RST. He was also told that the proscenium arch was holding up the building: remove it and the Company would end up with a large pile of bricks. 'We quite quickly moved on to the notion of demolition, of creating a new space. Then we went through whether we would keep the bits at the front – the Art Deco detail – or not. The die was cast at the interviews for the architect. We had arrived at a certain conclusion about a certain architect and then suddenly someone said, "Aren't we being a bit boring here? Aren't we just going to get a four-square new building? Shouldn't we be looking at something more interesting?"'

So the project team looked again at the architects interested in the job and the feeling was that if the Company wanted to go for a building that was bold and radical, it had to choose Erick van Egeraat. 'He had the most extraordinary imagination of the people we were interviewing. We plumped for Erick and the moment we had done that, it was virtually impossible to conceive of a building that kept the old Art Deco bits at the front.'

Noble believed then, and still believed when interviewed, that the clash with English Heritage was not a major problem. English Heritage, he suggested, tends not to make prescriptive statements. It gives opinions and advice but cannot tell local planners what they can and cannot do. Noble claimed that, in cases where English Heritage had opposed a scheme, promoters had challenged the decision and won, and gone on to change or demolish a listed building.

If, however, demolition of the RST was going to prove impossible, the new theatre would have to move across the road to the site of the Grade II listed Arden Hotel, leaving the old RST where it was. The Company would

The Art Deco fountain court in the RST

keep the shell of the RST, gut it and turn it into a continuously evolving found space. This idea derived from Noble's experience of directing his 1996 film of *A Midsummer Night's Dream*, when he had arranged for a replica Shakespearean theatre to be set in a void on a large soundstage.

'You would make a decision at the beginning of the year and create inside the brick shell of the RST a different space for each season and give to the future a whole raft of artistic opportunities. One season, say, we would have nothing in there at all, a completely empty-space promenade theatre for four Shakespeare plays. Another season we might want to explore new plays on a larger scale and so build a 400-seat theatre from scaffolding. All the people I consulted thought that was a fantastic idea. You would use the old shell as a resource and that would seem to be completely consonant with the way theatre was going in the 21st century.'

But not everyone agreed that it was a fantastic idea. The campaign to save the RST began to hot up and was followed by a new controversy, this time over the Shakespeare village, announced by the RSC in August 2001. 'I loathed the notion of the village but I was assured by all my advisers that it was a frightfully good idea. But I always thought it was a bit naff. As far as I was

The tin shed before the steel shed: the original The Other Place

concerned, the centre of our work was what happened on stage in the afternoons and evenings. Therefore you want to create optimum conditions for the performance of Shakespeare's plays. But without question, a company with the size, resources and traditions of the RSC could offer a breadth of opportunities and

I imagined we could create opportunities for young people that were completely different from anything we had been able to do before.'

Noble dismissed claims that he was wrong to leave the RSC at so critical a time to direct a commercial musical. He had, he said, taken no significant time off apart from five weeks to direct a Monteverdi opera in Aix-en-Provence; he had gone through the correct channels with the governors; he was still working for the RSC and had a good staff who could implement his new policies.

He was also accused of failing to consult within the RSC and Stratford, a charge he also rejected. His planned consultation would have come at a later point in the process rather than at the beginning, when what was required was leadership. 'I think a question about whether you want to demolish a building is a very hard one to take to consultation. Your experience tells you there are times when you have to take leadership and there are times when you have to consult widely.'

He acknowledged, however, that he had tried to do too much, too quickly, with too many changes in the Company happening at the same time. 'I have to take responsibility for that because I was the Chief Executive and I could have insisted that we have a different kind of timing. But I didn't. I don't think the policies were wrong on any front whatsoever. But I think the timings were totally wrong.'

As Chief Executive, should he not have foreseen the timing problem? 'Probably yes. I should have counselled a much slower approach. In my defence, I will say that I found myself quite isolated. In any situation like this, there is a triumvirate that runs a theatre company – a chairman, the chief executive and the managing director. In the triumvirate that happened during the redevelopment, I was the only person with any theatre experience whatsoever. Therefore the normal processes of checks and balances weren't in place. So it was me, me and me.'

After Noble left the Company in 2003 to direct plays and operas around the world, his successor Michael Boyd continued to argue that a new flexible theatre combining thrust stage and proscenium arch was a mirage. The Board realised it would have to decide between the Noble and Boyd visions and eventually opted to abandon any attempt at flexibility. Noble thinks that was a mistake.

He said he was far from convinced that it is right for Stratford to have three similar auditoriums in the RST, the Swan and The Other Place. 'My worry is the baby bear, mummy bear and daddy bear aspect. They will have three theatres that are exactly the same and have exactly the same relationship with the audience.'

In response, Boyd made it clear that he wanted nothing to do with daddy, mummy or baby bear and that Noble was wrong. 'The Other Place usually played end-on. So there is no baby bear; it's just daddy bear and mummy bear. Which then becomes a bad analogy, because I don't regard a daddy as more important than a mummy. But the RST is as sure as hell more important than the Swan. The logical conclusion of what Adrian claimed is that the Swan has found the most popular format in UK theatre – but the RST is not allowed to have it.

'We are made or broken in the end by our work in the RST. It is more important that the RST, rather than the

The RST entrance prior to Transformation

Swan, is a perfect auditorium for Shakespeare and Renaissance drama. If the Swan building were to be returned to its original proscenium form at some point in the future, it wouldn't bother me; it would be a nice wheel of history.

'We proved over four years that The Courtyard did not behave as the Swan does; it behaved in a very different way and so will the RST. We were quite spectacular with, for instance, the *Histories*, with *Romeo and Juliet* and with *Matilda*, mostly with bodies moving through space. That approach does not suit the Swan. Adrian's problem is superficial – the two theatres are not the same.' The Swan, he added, was a bare wooden space which directors and designers over-designed at their peril; it offered at its best an intense relationship between the actor, the words and the audience. But in the new RST designers and directors could learn how to create spectacle. 'To the extent that a thrust stage like that in the RST requires a plastic imagination and sculptural intelligence on the part of British theatre directors, then I am happy if it is a training ground for the future, for the art of the director.'

If Boyd's dismissal of Noble's scheme is based on a radically different theatrical vision, Sir Christopher Bland's is – with the benefit of hindsight – bluntly practical. 'Adrian's plan for Stratford was fatally flawed and had no chance of success. It involved the demolition of one Grade II* listed building, the first designed by a woman architect, and the Arden Hotel, part of which was also listed.

'English Heritage's opposition made a lengthy and expensive planning enquiry inevitable, with a successful outcome unlikely. There are very few instances of English Heritage's advice being disregarded in similar circumstances. And a role for and the continuing cost of the almost abandoned RST, had a new theatre been built, was, to put it politely, unclear.'

In July 2002, the RSC's Board, chaired by Lord Alexander of Weedon, appointed Michael Boyd to succeed Adrian Noble as the RSC's Artistic Director.

But Boyd had to wait in the wings while Noble worked out his notice period, during which the plan for an adaptable auditorium with both a proscenium arch and thrust stage lingered on: it would be on the site of the Arden Hotel and Erick van Egeraat would design it.

Boyd, however, was not an admirer of flexible theatres. He wanted to abandon any thoughts of a proscenium and commit the RSC unequivocally to a thrust stage auditorium within the Royal Shakespeare Theatre. By the time he took control of the Company in April 2003, he had had nine months to think about the future of the Royal Shakespeare Company, its £2.8 million deficit, a London base and what to do with the Royal Shakespeare Theatre. His ambitions were clear: the traditional RSC ensemble would be reinvented, the deficit would be addressed and the RST would not be handed over to the demolition men.

It would instead survive in an exciting new form.

The new auditorium begins to take shape

Boyd had not been close to the Noble project. 'The problem lay in an attempt to create a theatre that could be both proscenium and thrust,' he said. 'That's what sunk the early attempts, because it seemed to make a complete rebuild absolutely necessary. The argument was that an auditorium sufficiently large to contain both those possibilities made wholesale demolition of the entire RST almost inevitable. The received wisdom was that even if you were to go down to a thrust-only solution – which was never acceptable under the previous regime – there would still not be room for a sufficiently large auditorium to be economically viable. That was something I instinctively distrusted.'

Boyd also recoiled from the prospect of a new theatre on the Arden site. 'I began to imagine Stratford on Waterside and from Clopton Bridge with two huge buildings – the old RST and the new theatre on the Arden site – right next to each other. It felt architecturally overblown and its monumentalism worried me greatly.

'The other thing that worried me about building on the Arden site was a sort of voodoo – it wasn't by the river.

'The theatre is on an iconic site right by the Avon but we would not be doing our core repertoire – Shakespeare plays – there. It didn't feel right.'

Boyd's scheme to reconstruct the Royal Shakespeare Theatre in thrust stage format was conceived in secret in an unremarkable room somewhere in Stratford-upon-Avon. In the month Noble left and he became Artistic Director, he began to conspire with a computer and Flip Tanner, the former Technical Director of The Other Place, to try out hush-hush designs for a new auditorium that would fit within the walls of the RST and be built round a thrust stage. This was not official Royal Shakespeare Company policy; Boyd's plotting was cloak-and-dagger stuff worthy of a Shakespearean subplot.

A visualisation of the planned new RST auditorium

The clandestine sessions with the computer took on a new urgency as Boyd and Tanner began to investigate how many seats they could fit round a thrust stage between the RST's Art Deco foyer and the unmoveable fly tower. It would be a bit of a squeeze but they were convinced they could come up with a solution that would be economically viable. 'There came a critical moment when we got past 800 seats and people started to listen. When we nudged 900, people started to really listen,' said Boyd. 'When we reached 1,030 seats, people could see that the scheme was viable. Everyone began to unite round that idea.'

The walls come down: clearing space for the new auditorium

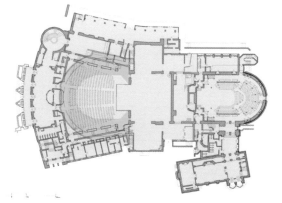

The new auditorium overlaid onto the plan of the 1932 building

The new RST scheme would preserve the ghosts in the old walls and solve the problems that had dogged Stratford's directors for generations. But there was an inherent paradox in this proposal: Boyd was determined to keep as the centre of Shakespeare production in

Stratford a theatre for which, as his thoughts after the final *Coriolanus* had shown, he had little affection. He respected the emotions of those old Company hands who had loved the RST but, left to his own devices, he would probably have been quite happy to have sat on a crane and swung a large wrecking ball at it.

'I didn't grow up here and the RSC was not the centre of my theatrical world in the 70s or 80s. I didn't have an emotional investment in that building apart from my working time here since the mid-90s. I didn't see Olivier as Coriolanus or Titus, or Vivien Leigh in any of her roles. I didn't even see Antony Sher's Richard III. My history was being a trainee director in Coventry when Stratford seemed like a cultural excrescence, an irrelevance 18 miles down the road. I was young and arrogant and Coventry was much more the centre of the cultural universe. I was probably unlucky in the Shakespeare that I came to see in those years. If I was attached to Stratford-upon-Avon at all, it was to The Other Place and the new plays I had seen.'

The experience of watching a play in the old RST with its barrier-like proscenium arch was 'like looking at a piece of theatre through the wrong end of a telescope with one group of people in a darkened room looking at another group of people in a brightly lit room through a hole in the wall. It now seems absurd. It wasn't when it evolved and it is still not when you are essentially creating beautiful two-dimensional pictures. Terrific – but it doesn't serve Shakespeare. In its DNA, his work involves a directness and an honesty of address with its audience that is so much more vividly served in an open staging than in a proscenium staging.'

It's clear Boyd was no fan of the old RST; his master-stroke was to realise that it could, with a radical makeover, become the theatre he dreamed of. His vision was of a new one-room auditorium in which directors and actors could show that the theatre experience in the right kind of large space could be just as involving as in the most modish black-box studio. 'Digital and web-based interactive material seemed to me to be

New meets old. The RST auditorium takes shape within the walls of the old building

The amplifier area beneath the RST stage prior to Transformation. The amp racks are raised off the floor in case of flooding

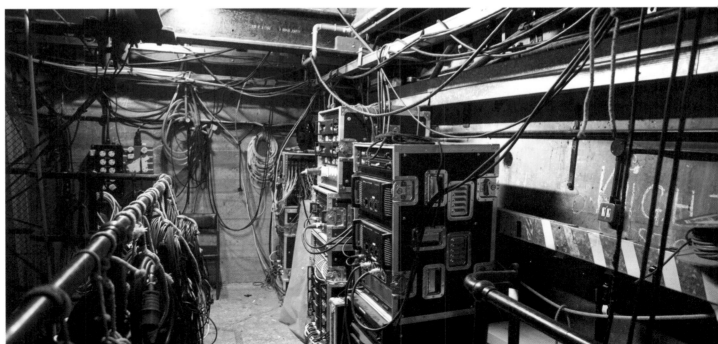

pushing theatre into an area of very small-scale, site-specific work that could involve a very intimate exchange with the audience and that could undeniably be an event that engaged people and was interactive. The fully felt human presence was at its most vivid, which is one of those things that define theatre against other art forms.

'But there seemed to be a retreat from large-scale work that was fully in the culture. There is always a danger of those site-specific works becoming deeply elitist and populated by fur coats because ticket availability is extremely limited. If you are going to enter the culture with theatre and take your place properly at the top table of art forms, you have to be able to do it on a larger scale.'

What Boyd was searching for was what he calls 'the crowded secular complicity of the Renaissance stage' but there was no precise theatrical model to copy. One influence was the Assembly Rooms in Edinburgh, where Tyrone Guthrie created his famous production of Sir David Lindsay's *A Satyre of the Thrie Estates* in 1948. Guthrie was the great advocate of the thrust stage but the theatres in which he was directly involved (Stratford, Ontario; Minneapolis) had open stages surrounded by a single sweep of seats.

Boyd wanted something different. He admired the Tricycle in London and, of course, the RSC's own Swan, whose positives were offset by some unexpected negatives. 'It was terribly important for the RSC to be able to attract leading theatre artists – actors and designers and directors – to want to work with us. We had a reasonably long queue of directors wanting to work in the RST but the queue to work at the Swan was a mile long. That eventually led to a much higher hit rate for work in the Swan than in the RST where I could see, when I was an Associate Director, the reputation of that theatre going down.

'The RSC's reputation stands or falls on its Shakespeare

Curtain call for *Henry IV, Part II*, part of the *Histories* cycle in The Courtyard

work, no matter what else we do with contemporary and international work. The priority had to be to make the new theatre the place where everyone would want to work, where we would do our core Shakespeare repertoire. Above everything else I had to create a queue to work there.'

So there was no direct inspiration for the new RST. 'The idea of a pack 'em in and stack 'em high theatre on a large scale was slightly without precedent. There was the Globe, but that is very wide and very dependent on the idea of an audience that stands. There were the sacred arenas of the Greeks and their modern descendants – the Olivier, Chichester, the Crucible. I'm fond of them all in different ways but none has consistently proved to be a space with great tension, excitement, atmosphere. And there was the Shakespearean inn courtyard.'

Those were the influences. But in The Courtyard the RSC eventually had something much more significant: a prototype that had won acclaim from audiences, actors and critics and shown that Boyd's insistence on his preferred form of stage had been vindicated. If that collective enthusiasm could follow the RSC down the road and back into the new-look RST, the Company would have fulfilled Boyd's dominant aspiration: to present Shakespeare's plays in his own town in the auditorium best suited to them.

By the time the RSC was ready to launch its plans for the reconstruction of the RST, the Company had found architects who had come up with a plan that would give a large audience an intimate relationship with actors before them. At a media briefing at the Royal Institute of British Architects in June 2006, Boyd revealed that the seat furthest from the action in the new auditorium would be 15 metres away from the stage, compared with 27 metres in the old RST. 'Crudely,' he added, 'the auditorium brings the audience close to the actors

so that they can see right up their nostrils and the particular shape of their eye muscles.'

Some have questioned Boyd's certainty that there was no alternative to the design that emerged from those secret sessions with a computer. 'I have been told repeatedly on this journey that it is very unwise of me to commit Stratford to a thrust stage. Some have asked where would we tour, where would we transfer in London?

'But I have always been very clear that if you get the central issue right, the rest will sort itself out.'

Media briefing at the RIBA in June 2006

Towards the end of 2003 Boyd began his campaign to convince members of the RSC's Board to support his two unshakeable convictions:

that the new theatre should be unequivocally thrust stage and could and should be created within the walls of the Royal Shakespeare Theatre.

His plan was supported by Vikki Heywood, appointed the RSC's Interim Executive Director in September 2003, who was also less than keen on the plan for a new theatre on the Arden Hotel site. 'The Arden option had come on to the table because the Company had to have somewhere it could perform while the RST was redeveloped,' she said. 'But what does the old theatre become once you have built the new one? No one could come up with a really good alternative plan for what that building should be.'

Heywood, a former stage manager at Stratford, had previously been Chief Executive at the Royal Court Theatre in London where she had overseen a reconstruction project that ended in 2000; she then spent a couple of years as a freelance consultant. In September 2003, Boyd asked her to join the Company

The Courtyard Theatre:
preliminary sketch by
Charcoalblue

while it searched for a new executive director. 'The idea was that I would come for six months and leave again. I had just done a huge capital project at the Royal Court and I was very sure of one thing – I wasn't going to do another one. I had been brought in earlier in 2003 by Arts Council England as part of a group to advise on how it should approach the RSC scheme. So I had got to know a bit about the problems the Company was facing.'

Her resolution crumbled. She ended up applying for and winning the permanent post and joined the Company as Sir Christopher Bland, then Chairman of British Telecom, took over as Chairman of the RSC Board. He too was unimpressed by the plan for a replacement for the RST. 'Fairly soon after I arrived, there was still a view that maybe we would knock down the RST and rebuild there or build another theatre on the site of the Arden hotel,' said Bland. 'It was nonsense.'

Meanwhile, the RSC's governing structure had gone through a revolution. In the late 1990s, a group of governors led by Sir Geoffrey Cass, who had been Chair of the Company's Board since 1985, rewrote the Royal Charter that set out the RSC's corporate governance structure. The outdated and unwieldy system then current had allowed for 75 governors who met once a year; from that group a council of 25-26 members was drawn and met twice a year. There were no clear terms of office.

The restructured system, presented by Cass and approved by the Privy Council, provided for a group of 45 governors from whom a Board of up to 20 would be drawn. Now the Board is usually kept to a maximum of 16 and acts more like a PLC board with people with relevant skills. Terms of office were introduced and standing committees set up. The new slimmer and fleeter Board met for the first time in 2000 and had settled into more efficient ways of working by the time Boyd began deploying all his persuasive skills.

Cass was succeeded by Lord Alexander of Weedon, who chaired the RSC's Board for just three years but managed the handover from Adrian Noble to Michael Boyd, and then supported Boyd in his plan to reform the RSC as an ensemble company.

By early 2004 Lord Alexander had stepped down and the slimmed-down Board began to accept that a new theatre was not the best solution to the Company's problems in Stratford. But there was a major snag: the RSC still had a contract with architect Erick van Egeraat to design a completely new theatre. If the Board was not yet totally certain about what it was going to do, it came to a clear conclusion about what it was not going to do. On 27 May 2004 the RSC issued a press release: 'Erick van Egeraat Associated Architects (EEA London Ltd) and the Royal Shakespeare Company are confirming today that they have, by mutual agreement, terminated their collaboration on the redevelopment of the RSC's theatres in Stratford-upon-Avon.'

So ended a relationship that had lasted seven years. Van Egeraat told *The Independent* that the project needed an 'unrestricted rethinking'; the RSC said that demolition of the theatre was now 'less likely'.

As van Egeraat and the RSC bade farewell to each other, Boyd and Tanner concluded that the only way to make the new auditorium fit within the RST footprint was to remove the load-bearing side walls of the old one; and if those walls came down, the roof would have to come off too. This unthinkable strategy – to which English Heritage would have to subscribe – gradually achieved acceptance among many who had come to realise that the RST was not quite as beautiful and inviolable as they had always thought. Boyd's scheme, a pragmatic compromise that would blend old and new, was clearly preferable to wholesale demolition.

Bland, keen to establish with certainty what could and could not be done to the RST, then suggested a meeting with Simon Thurley, who had been appointed Chief Executive of English Heritage in 2002.

'I said we should go to English Heritage and ask them about their position on the theatre,'

said Bland. 'Vikki and Susie [Sainsbury] were there and the meeting lasted barely 20 minutes. They [English Heritage] said, "This is a Grade II* listed building. If you apply for planning permission to demolish it, we will oppose it. We will go to inquiry, we will win, you'll waste three years and £3 million. We will tell you the bits we mind about." As indeed they did.'

Thurley or one of his officials then produced a plan of the theatre and coloured in the bits that had to stay – the Art Deco foyer, the fountain court and the façades facing the Bancroft Gardens and the Avon. 'They said, "As far as the rest is concerned, do what you like",' said Bland. 'The building was not fit for purpose; it was absolutely clapped out.

'English Heritage were very clear and after that we were very clear. From that moment on, total demolition and a brand new theatre was never a runner.'

 Façade of the 1932 theatre, with sculpture panels by Eric Kennington

Thurley and his team advised the RSC that, if they found the plans to remodel the RST satisfactory, they would not oppose the RSC's wish to remove the roof of the theatre and demolish the auditorium's internal walls and the wall on to Waterside. Previous English Heritage advice had been that that was not an option. (Four years later, English Heritage was to hail the RST reconstruction scheme as 'exemplary'.)

'It was an absolutely crucial meeting,' Heywood remembered. 'Simon was quite new and very brave. We are indebted to him because if he had wobbled at that moment that would have started a wobble among everyone else that could not have been stopped. Simon said he thought it was exactly the right thing to do. That was a change from conversations that had happened with English Heritage in the past. Simon was brilliant at realising that just saying no meant saying no to the whole project.'

The official English Heritage line was eventually published on its website: 'An analysis of the [RST], following English Heritage's guidelines, provided an objective understanding of its historic significance. The analysis demonstrated that it was possible to replace the auditorium without damaging historically significant features of the building, such as the Art Deco foyer, that justified its listing.' Which is perhaps a polite way of saying that, apart from the foyer, the fountain court and the Bancroft and riverside façades, the building was not up to much and did not need to be granted too much respect.

On 22 September 2004, a month or so after the meeting with Thurley, the RSC's Board met to consider a report from its redevelopment committee that laid out three options: do nothing; create a new auditorium within

November 2007: the roof comes off the RST

The Art Deco foyer
in 2006

and in 1932

the RST; or build a new theatre on the Arden site. The committee, chaired by Susie Sainsbury, firmly recommended option two. Sainsbury explained that she had previously been in favour of creating a totally new Royal Shakespeare Theatre but had changed her mind, convinced 'by the artistic argument in favour of keeping the best of the past while moving forward'.

It was time for the Board to make up its mind. Members voted unanimously in favour of option two and resolved to examine a brief for architects at their next meeting. The Transformation project was under way.

The other good news was that Arts Council England eventually accepted that the RSC could not simultaneously work on plans for theatres in both London and Stratford. It also accepted that the Company now planned to create in Stratford a kind of theatre that did not exist in London.

The way was clear for the Royal Shakespeare Company to press ahead with its second attempt at creating a new home. The former architect and Artistic Director had departed and with them had gone a plan that had proved impractical to realise. In had come a new Chair of a reconstructed Board, a new Executive Director, a new Artistic Director and a new plan. The future was looking bright: all the RSC had to do was make this second scheme work.

But the Company was still licking its wounds. 'The mood was a very odd combination of excitement and exhaustion,' said Heywood. 'There was a huge amount of goodwill for what Michael was talking about. While staff felt somewhat shell-shocked and very tired because they had just been through a very scary experience, there was a sense that the organisation was about to get back in control of itself and its destiny. When I arrived, there were two simultaneous emotions: one was that

staff felt they could not cope with any more change because they had just gone through an enormous amount of it; the other was a huge appetite for change because they wanted to get behind Michael. So it was all quite odd.

'Company members were very frightened of plans because the RSC had never really had a formal plan before. It had then had a big plan that had not been very well consulted and had been effectively imposed on the organisation. That plan had gone phenomenally wrong. The idea of planning was something that people were very anxious about although they desperately wanted a structure in their lives. We started to introduce the idea that there was going to be quite a long-distance plan and that everyone was going to work on it together.

'By the time the plan was produced, everyone felt that it was something they owned.'

And then in the autumn of 2004, almost exactly a year after she took up the job, Heywood, with Boyd, had a bright idea that became crucial to the success of the whole Transformation project.

The Royal Shakespeare Company had finally decided on the theatre it wanted.

But it could not afford to lose a major performance space for the three years or more that it would take to reshape the RST: that would have meant economic disaster for both the Company and Stratford.

So the emerging scheme included a plan for a so-called transitional theatre that would open in 2007 as the RSC's principal Stratford venue when work began on the RST and the Swan. But Heywood and Boyd suggested late in 2004 that construction should be brought forward a year: the new theatre could then open in 2006 to provide a third auditorium for the *Complete Works* Festival, one of the most exciting projects in the Company's history. The RSC's Board embraced the idea; the as yet unnamed theatre would cease to be a mere understudy and would play a leading role in the *Complete Works*. Susie Sainsbury described the idea as

extremely brave, not to say batty.

What made the scheme particularly sensitive as well as batty was that the new theatre would rise in the form of a steel shed in the midst of a clutch of listed buildings in a conservation area and within yards of an iconic English river bank and Holy Trinity, Stratford's 800-year-old parish church.

'The marketeer in me knew we would have resistance to the temporary theatre and that we needed to get through that resistance before we reached the point where we

The Courtyard Theatre, rising above the chain ferry, begins to change from grey to warm red

The framework for The Courtyard rises on The Other Place car park

were entirely reliant on it financially,' said Heywood. 'We had to get the audience to experience the theatre and like it before we shut down the RST. We needed their purchasing power.' The Company's artists would also have an extra year to get used to the thrust stage and

Boyd and his team would be able to learn many crucial lessons for the new RST.

The benefits of bringing forward construction were spelled out in the design statement that accompanied the planning application eventually submitted to Stratford-on-Avon District Council. 'It is the RSC's intention that the auditorium will be a prototype for the new Royal Shakespeare Theatre, allowing the Company to test and experiment with a new one-room thrust stage,' wrote Michael Boyd. 'It avoids having the audiences "sit in a waiting room" until the new theatre is built but instead provides them with an exciting new, large-scale theatre.'

Elsewhere, the statement suggested that the *Complete Works* Festival would be 'a major opportunity to put the theatre on the map, casting out any doubt in the public's mind that the continuity of the RSC's performances in Stratford might be disrupted during the redevelopment of the Royal Shakespeare Theatre'.

The *Complete Works* project, suggested by Boyd and approved by the Board in 2004, was almost as batty as the scheme for a temporary theatre. (The building became known as The Courtyard Theatre in March 2005 after planning permission had been granted.) 'It was incredibly brave, not to say foolhardy, of Michael to suggest that we do it at the same time as we were going through everything else,' said Sir Christopher Bland. 'We were still recovering from a couple of years of deficit and we were looking at the whole business of raising money for the new theatre, getting planning permission for it and getting The Courtyard built. To do the *Complete Works*

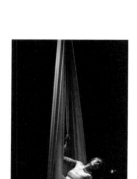

Tim Supple's Indian
*A Midsummer Night's
Dream* from the
Complete Works Festival

on top of that was bold to the point of rashness. We felt we could do it – although we were not quite clear how. We had quite enough on our plate but we said we should do it.'

Bland suggested that Boyd deserved great credit for coming up with the idea and persuading the Board to do it; the Board also deserved credit for realising how important the scheme could be in re-establishing the reputation of the RSC.

There was no doubt that bringing forward construction of the transitional theatre would be a good thing and the issue was first raised at a Board meeting in October 2004 attended by architect Ian Ritchie, an RSC governor. Ritchie spelled out a few stark facts: he worked backwards from summer 2006, when the new theatre would have to be ready, and explained that any plans would have to be approved by the Board before Christmas 2004 – that is, within about ten weeks. The rush was necessary because Stratford-on-Avon District Council would have to grant planning permission by early April 2005 if the theatre was to stand a chance of opening on time. 'That would leave only a year to build the theatre, which I thought was the minimum time necessary,' said Ritchie.

As Board members considered this prospect, a short but significant conversation took place. 'Could it be done?' asked Bland.

'I could do it,' replied Ritchie.

RSC folklore suggests that Ritchie then left the meeting, went back to his office and made a preliminary sketch on the back of a napkin.

It showed in minimal form a very long curtain being drawn around a rectangular space. The sketch certainly existed: it features on the title page of the book on The Courtyard produced by Ian Ritchie's practice and a print of it hangs in Vikki Heywood's office.

But rather than immediately after the board meeting, Ritchie had put pencil to paper some weeks before and in a black notebook rather than on a napkin. 'I had been approached before the board meeting and did a bit of thinking, so I did not go to Stratford completely unprepared.'

Ritchie had also worked out in advance what the temporary building would cost. The Noble/van Egeraat scheme had also included a plan for a temporary theatre: it would have had up to 650 seats and cost £12 million. Ritchie said he could build a theatre half as big again (1,050 seats) for half the price: his calculations were based on his experience of building a theatre in France, which had cost £4,000 a seat. 'Allowing for inflation, I said we could do it for around £5,000 a seat,' he said. 'It's a wonderful moment when people ask you if you can do something like this. You say yes – and they believe you.'

Ritchie, who had also drawn up plans for a temporary auditorium at Tower Bridge in London to be used during the renovation of the Royal Opera House (it was never built), came up with a scheme that was beautifully simple: he would design for the car park of The Other Place a

Ian Ritchie's preliminary sketch for The Courtyard Theatre

The Other Place (left) and a visualisation of how The Courtyard would slot into place (right)

plain, rectangular box using sheets of folded COR-TEN steel, a material often used for shoring up canal banks but probably never before for a theatre. When delivered, the steel would be grey; it would then rust to a bright orange before turning a warm red to match the colour of much of Stratford's Midlands red brick. (Ritchie likes rust. 'I call it nature's own paintbrush,' he once said.) When the theatre had come to the end of its temporary run in the limelight, all that steel could be recycled.

Within the rusty box would sit the thrust stage and the freestanding auditorium, nothing more: all other services – bars, shop, toilets, dressing rooms, laundry – would be in The Other Place, which would abandon its own theatrical ambitions for a few years. Its plain, square auditorium would be divided in half by a new floor with a square section cut out so that audiences could look up and down at each other.

Ritchie's slim volume on The Courtyard set out his own 'rules of engagement'. (God was happy with 10 commandments; Ritchie laid down 13.) 'Design should be simple so that it could be delivered on time; design everything, inside the budget; design it for theatre, actor-audience – not for the ego of the architect; design it to be great, not just good; always make decisions to favour the theatrical experience; create spaces that allow full expression of the theatrical values of the RSC; create an auditorium space that is a total experience, not just

a stage; remember why and for whom it is being done; remember the client's audience is from Stratford, London, the rest of the world, and of all ages; a theatre is for live performers in front of a live audience – all want to experience it; work with people to earn their respect; it is the job not your job that matters; if in doubt, don't. Find and ask the person with the best knowledge.'

The priority was the delivery on time of a theatre that worked; if fine architecture were also delivered, that would be a bonus. 'I designed a box and separated it from the auditorium to buy us time to design the theatre inside it. I kept things simple,' said Ritchie.

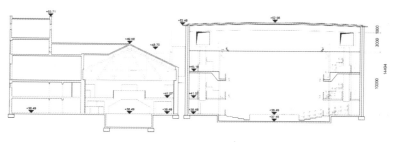

Cross section of The Courtyard Theatre adjoining The Other Place

Ritchie's plans, drawn up within six weeks, for The Courtyard and the conversion of The Other Place were submitted to Stratford-on-Avon District Council just before the Christmas break; the RSC needed a decision by April at the latest to allow necessary groundwork to start. Ritchie had already said that the steel for the building would need to be ordered before planning permission was granted: the Company was living dangerously. This frantic rush did not seem to faze Boyd:

'Theatre is a deadline profession. We have opening nights,' he said.

The steel framework of The Courtyard Theatre

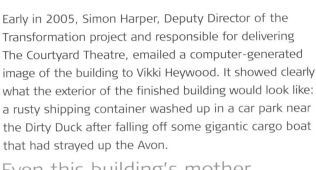

Early in 2005, Simon Harper, Deputy Director of the Transformation project and responsible for delivering The Courtyard Theatre, emailed a computer-generated image of the building to Vikki Heywood. It showed clearly what the exterior of the finished building would look like: a rusty shipping container washed up in a car park near the Dirty Duck after falling off some gigantic cargo boat that had strayed up the Avon.

'Even this building's mother wouldn't say it was beautiful,'
wrote Harper in an accompanying note.

The steel box stirred up fierce controversy in Stratford because little time was available for consultation; opponents described Ritchie's building as a carbuncle, a blot on the landscape and a diabolical eyesore. 'The meetings on the temporary space were horrible, especially with residents, because the scheme was so quick,' said Roger Mortlock, then the RSC's Director of Communications. 'Construction had a real impact on the lives of people who lived in Avonbank Paddocks [adjacent to The Courtyard site].'

In 1870, the *Stratford-upon-Avon Herald* had announced in just three paragraphs the plan to build a Shakespeare Memorial Theatre; in 2004-5, the paper gave rather more space to The Courtyard story. 'There was a huge row and this is where the conspiracy theory and distrust manifested itself,' said Chris Towner, the *Herald's* editor. 'There was a feeling that if the RSC wanted this temporary theatre to be made permanent, then it would be made permanent. I don't think Michael Boyd was ever able to convince the really suspicious people that the RSC did not want two 1,000-seat theatres in Stratford.'

The Courtyard's fate would be decided at a meeting of the council's area planning committee on 10 March at which councillors would be asked to give planning

The Courtyard seen from the Ashcroft Room above the Swan Theatre

permission that would last until 31 March 2010, when the theatre would fade away like Bottom's dream; The Other Place would then be restored to its original form. The RSC high command turned out in force, sitting in the front row of the public gallery. 'It was quite scary because I wasn't really sure how councillors were going to respond,' said Heywood. 'We had a feeling that they would have the sense to go for it but it was a challenging planning application.'

'Ian Ritchie was very confident that we would get planning permission,' said Susie Sainsbury. 'I wasn't half as sanguine as he was. It was absolutely terrifying. The council had a special meeting for it. We nearly lost it.'

'We assumed that we would get temporary planning permission,' said Bland. 'But we jolly nearly didn't. I was scowling. It was terrifying because if that decision had gone the wrong way, the whole sequence of events and timing would have been set back very seriously. If we didn't have the temporary theatre, none of the other bits of the jigsaw made much sense. We would have to do something else – get a big tent or delay everything for 10 years. It was all fairly scary.'

So scary that Jane Ellis, the RSC's Communications Manager, thought she was going to be sick. 'I think sitting in a planning committee meeting is probably one of the most nerve-racking things I have ever done.'

The *Stratford-upon-Avon Herald* covered this major story at length and in style. 'The public gallery was packed to overflowing,' wrote Preston Witts in a colourful report that could have been headlined To Be Or Not To Be. 'The atmosphere was tense. The minutes ticked away. And then the silence that fell in the moments approaching 6pm was shattered by the resounding thud of the chairman's gavel. One of the most important meetings in Stratford's history had just begun . . . The central area planning committee was taking a decision that would make or break the organisation bearing the name of the greatest playwright of all time.'

Stratford's planning officers had recommended that, even though it contravened local planning rules, the scheme should be approved because of its economic and cultural significance to the town and the region. But the council's own conservation architect said The Courtyard was 'grossly overscaled for its sensitive location, overpowering the listed buildings' and other local opponents joined in the attack. Kevin Gildea, who kept a particularly close watch on both The Courtyard and RST schemes, told councillors: 'This scheme breaks your own rules. It is grossly overpowering the listed buildings. Future planning control will be undermined if this goes ahead.'

In recommending the scheme to the council, Vikki Heywood said: 'Our proposal safeguards the prosperity of the town and keeps Stratford on the map.

'It is a wonderful opportunity to tell the whole world about Stratford.'

But councillors were determined to have their say. One wanted more consultation and investigation of other sites; others were worried about traffic in Southern Lane; and Councillor Lynda Organ sent chills down the spines of Heywood and her colleagues when she suggested that work on The Courtyard should not begin until planning permission had been granted for the new RST. This move, designed to ensure that The Courtyard did not live on beyond its 2010 deadline because of building delays at the reconstructed theatre, would have wrecked the timetable for the Transformation project.

'There is great concern that this temporary structure will not be coming down in 2010,' she told the committee. 'I think we should do everything to make sure this happens.' Her proposal won no support. (The structure did not come down in March 2010: in 2009, the RSC secured an uncontroversial extension until 31 December 2012.)

After almost two hours, the proposal to approve the scheme went to the vote. 'Hands went up and the chairman swiftly announced "Granted",' reported Witts. 'Smiles came from Sir Christopher [Bland] and the RSC team as the public gallery began to empty.' Five councillors voted in favour, one against, and planning permission was granted with 13 conditions, two of them added by members at the meeting. One insisted

that the word 'temporary' should precede the word 'theatre' whenever the new building was mentioned.

As the meeting wound up, very relieved members of the RSC's high command moved on to Lambs restaurant in Sheep Street for dinner. Although Heywood insisted that this was not to be a triumphant celebration, Bland ordered a bottle or two of champagne. 'And what's the occasion?' asked the smiling waiter as he removed the first cork. Aware of Heywood's strictures, Bland paused for only a moment before announcing that he was marrying Michele Percy, the clerk to the RSC's governors.

The next day, a letter went from Michael Boyd to the RSC members to tell them the good news. Five weeks after the planning meeting, the RSC signed a contract with Dutch contractors ZNS Van Dam Geveltechniek BV. In May, the Company signed a second contract with AMEC, an international project management and services company, for the conversion of The Other Place.

Within weeks, four of the Dutch company's steel erectors set to work and the rusty walls and roof were in place by the end of 2005. At that stage, the building, carefully watched over by Rui Dias, Project Director for Ian Ritchie Architects, had the look of a lofty hangar, somewhere you might service a small Boeing, or a factory, somewhere for the manufacture of mighty lengths of chain.

It certainly did not look like a space where words might take wing.

 Final adjustments to the steelwork of The Courtyard's roof

INTERVAL 01.

Clay as grey as a winter morning slithers through an upscaled sausage machine, exits through a spout and forms itself into a dollop the shape of a birthday cake. The clod is stacked on a pallet and then taken to a high table in a long shed where it waits its turn to be transformed.

Eventually it is picked up by one of six strong-armed men (and one strong-armed woman), pummelled, rolled in sand and, with unerring aim, walloped into a rectangular wooden mould, the excess clay whisked away with a giant cheese wire. Each of these throwers can produce a perfectly brick-shaped lump of clay every 20 seconds and by the end of a productive shift may have stacked up 1,600 of them.

'You have to be strong enough and skilled enough to do the job and have the ability to shut off while doing something so repetitive for such long periods of time,' says Huw Gilson, Director of Coleford Brick & Tile of Cinderford in the Forest of Dean.

Gilson's company has made 168,000 bricks for the Royal Shakespeare Company: some for the reconstruction of the Royal Shakespeare Theatre, some for the new tower. Many are of a standard size with the usual indentation called, for no clear reason, a frog; about 14,000 were bespoke, specially made to suit the odd shapes and sizes demanded by architects Bennetts Associates, particularly for repairs to the RST's riverside façade and for the three-degree slope on the tower. 'We excel in the unusual,' adds Gilson proudly. 'We are lucky: our clay is very suitable for making bricks of intricate shapes and sizes.'

Bennetts had flirted with Dutch or German bricks but eventually found their way to Coleford, one of only a handful of British companies still making bricks in the traditional way a medieval builder might recognise. The company, founded 80 years ago, was bought by the Gilson family in 2003 and has since supplied bricks – Mixed Purples, Vauxhall Greys, Cotswold Buffs, Dark Bedford Multis and the rest – to English Heritage and the National Trust for restoration projects.

But most of Coleford's annual stack of 1.5 million bricks are now ordered by architects for prestige buildings: elegant private homes with exuberant chimneys; corporate headquarters; Oxbridge colleges (Keble, Clare, Selwyn); Rick Mather's extension to the Ashmolean Museum in Oxford; a large mosque in Cardiff; and now one of the world's most famous theatres. 'Architects have been through the concrete phase and are still in their glass façade phase,' says Gilson. 'Fortunately bricks are coming back into fashion. Architects are looking for something different. They also like to challenge us to make bricks in various sizes and shapes and we are able to give them the dimensions and detail they want.'

The Coleford bricks have found favour because they look beautiful, do the job and ensure that the RST will probably still be standing when Shakespeare (who used the word brick or bricks only three times in his entire output) celebrates his 1,000th birthday in 2564. Coleford bricks are very hard and have the high compressive strength (>49N/mm2, for those who know what that means) needed to ensure that the RST's tower does not buckle at the knees. They do not suffer from frost damage or from efflorescence caused by powdery deposits of salts. They are also happy to sit underwater, which is why British Waterways uses them for canal repairs.

They do not come cheap. In 2009, you could buy a thousand decent machine-made bricks for £200; a thousand standard Coleford handmade bricks would have set you back £750. 'For most people, a brick is just a brick; but our bricks give a building integrity,' says Gilson. 'You get a warm, fuzzy feeling when you know that your building's bricks have been handmade.'

Perhaps in years to come audiences will be found stroking the RST's walls as they stock up on warm fuzziness before entering the theatre to see *Twelfth Night* or *Macbeth*. Fuzzy or not, it's the quality of the Forest of Dean clay that gives the bricks their aesthetic and practical virtues. The clay, which sits on top of the coal seams worked by the region's Free Miners, is dug from pits just 150 metres from the brick factory. A major dig takes place every six years and the clay is carted to the Coleford works and laid in horizontal layers until it rises like a cliff face. The clay is removed in vertical cross sections to ensure uniform consistency.

A load is dropped into a feeder box and taken by conveyor belt to the pan, which resembles a vast mixing bowl in an industrial cake-making plant. Inside, two large milling stones rotate and crush the clay, to which water and barium (which limits the movement of soluble salts) have been added, to ensure that particle size is consistent in each clod. The clay moves on another conveyor to pass between mangle-like high-speed rollers prevented from kissing by a gap no bigger than three millimetres. After that, it travels into the pug (or sausage machine) to be extruded.

Then the throwers move into action, using the strength in their forearms to throw the clay. 'Not everyone can do it,' suggests Gilson. 'Some of our throwers are large and well-built; others are as thin as a piece of string. You have to develop a rhythm, a method of doing the job in a uniform way.'

The thrown bricks, which acquire their varied shades from the sand in which they are rolled, are all described as green until they are fired. As fast as a thrower throws, a bearer-offer takes the bricks and stacks them on a drying frame known as a stillage. Drying is crucial because a considerable amount of water is added to the clay to make it malleable: a standard green brick will be 17 per cent larger than a ready-to-use brick and will shrink from a hefty 4kg to a more manageable 2.7kg after firing.

The bricks sit on the stillages for a couple of days and lose some moisture naturally. Then they are placed in a gas-powered dryer in which the temperature rises from a little light warming to a blistering 200°C. 'You have to take a lot of the moisture out of the brick before you can put it in the kiln,' says Gilson. 'Otherwise it will crack, split or pop. The brick reduces in size all the time as it dries.'

When dried, the bricks have enough strength to be stacked (by hand; no fork-lifts) 16 units high in the kilns. One takes 12,000, the other 14,000 bricks; both resemble spacious, if over-warm, tents. The heat is turned on and raised to 1,100°C, at which point the bricks glow white-hot and almost vitrify. Once they are cool, they are drawn from the kiln and stacked on pallets; they do not hang around in the Coleford yard for long and most are sold even before they are made.

Now the blending process begins. This is where different shades of brick are mixed to create an overall palette, a process as subtle as with the finest paint. Individual shades, such as the Wessex Mixture, are not uniform in colour (no one wants a blank wall made up of identically coloured bricks) but full of subtle variation. Further shades can then be added to the blend to produce still more variations in colour and texture. The mix used for the Royal Shakespeare Theatre and its tower has become known as the Stratford Blend, an attractive melange of the Wessex Mixture, the Saxon Multi and the Forest Royal Mixed.

The Stratford Blend is made still more distinctive by using a smooth, rather than the more usual rough-textured, version of the Forest Royal. So what is seen at the theatre now is, appropriately enough, a world première of a new blend of brick. It's estimated that the original Elisabeth Scott theatre used 10 types of brick. Now an eleventh, handmade in a long shed just 55 miles from Stratford, has been added.

RSC
ROYAL
SHAKESPEARE
COMPANY
TRANSFORMING OUR
THEATRES
APPEAL
www.rsc.org.uk/appeal

Susie Hurley made her first visit to the RST in 1984, to see *Henry V* when it was Kenneth Branagh's turn to hurl himself into the breach. She was 17 and travelled to Stratford with her boyfriend on a bus from Reading.

They couldn't afford to stay anywhere so spent the night on a concrete bench in the alcove leading up to the balcony.

'It was so uncomfortable and, to combat the freezing cold and boredom, my boyfriend carried out a touching act of vandalism by carving our names into one of the bricks,' Hurley confessed. 'We later married and had two daughters and, although he and I are no longer together,

Members of the 2008-9 acting company lend their support to the appeal

each time I've visited Stratford since then I have made sure to visit my brick,

often with my daughter Katie who has inherited my love of the RST.'

Hurley's brick with its inscription is still there (it's about five feet up on a pillar) and she atoned for the vandalism by sending £50 to the RSC's Sponsor a Brick campaign. In *Henry VI, Part II*, Shakespeare suggests that bricks can be alive with memory; he would probably have relished the notion of a love token carved on a playhouse wall in the middle of a midsummer night and might have turned Hurley's story into a sonnet.

Fundraising was a major part of the Transformation project

By November 2010 more than 18,000 people from 60 countries had supported the Transformation appeal.

But neither the sale of bricks and seats (campaigns headed respectively by Sir Patrick Stewart and David Tennant), nor the rattling of buckets by actors after a performance of *Romeo and Juliet* in The Courtyard (the collection raised £1,200), nor top-up donations secured from patrons by gently persuasive box office staff could have provided all the cash needed. The RSC's Board and senior staff had to find the rest.

This was never going to be easy but it would have been much harder only a few years later, when big Lottery grants were a thing of the past and the world was gripped by financial chaos.

Until the early 1990s, many subsidised arts organisations regarded fundraising as an embarrassing concept that was beneath their dignity. The RSC was no different and, like many others, had to become much more sophisticated and professional in its approach to finding money from sources other than the public purse. Liam Fisher-Jones was appointed the Company's Director of Development in 1996 and stayed for 11 years, building up a team of 15 fundraisers before handing over to Caroline Jones, fresh from raising cash for the Young Vic. The growing team was, at least initially, viewed with suspicion by some Company members as spendthrifts who used RSC money to wine and dine potential donors and had little to do with the core business of putting on plays. Perceptions soon changed; they had to.

In 1999 the RSC, then still committed to Erick van Egeraat's new, flexible theatre, confidently applied to Arts Council England for a £25 million National Lottery

Sir Patrick Stewart, championing the Sponsor a Brick initiative

Executive Director Vikki Heywood in fundraising mode

capital grant. But the Council said no. This was at a time when some major Lottery-funded projects were in trouble, notably the National Centre for Popular Music in Sheffield, to which ACE had given £11 million. Bad news Lottery stories were attracting grim headlines.

Moss Cooper, then head of the Council's Lottery Fund, told the RSC its scheme was not good enough; its corporate structure had to be overhauled and its management strengthened. It also had to come up with a plan to show where it would stage plays while a new theatre was being built.

Cooper said he would not hand over £25 million but would make available twice that sum once the Company had sorted itself out and come up with what he called 'a damned good scheme'; £50 million was what he estimated the RSC needed to do the job properly.

No Arts Council England money had been handed over by the time Adrian Noble resigned in 2002. Concerned about the state of the Company, the Council sought advice the following year from what became known as its 'parliament', a group of consultants (including Vikki Heywood, then a freelance) sent in to examine the RSC's condition. The group advised the Council to back off and give the RSC time to regroup and get its house in order.

When the RSC Board decided in 2004 to create its new auditorium within the old RST, the thrust stage outline scheme was costed at £100 million, a price tag determined not so much by totting up the price of bricks and mortar but by Arts Council England's £50 million offer: the Board thought a matching £50 million would be about as much as it could raise from public and private donors.

Fundraising then became something bigger than finding lots of cash; it became a significant part of the recovery from a crisis that had threatened the Company's existence. In looking for money, the RSC found both friends it didn't know it had and also a unifying common purpose; the future began to look exciting. 'We had to show that the Company was uniting behind the scheme,' said Heywood. 'Previously, redevelopment had been seen as something that was being done to the RSC rather than by the RSC.'

The Company began to ensure that it was sending out unambiguous messages: the wobbles of the past were over and the RSC was back on form; it had a firm plan for a new auditorium and a temporary theatre; there was going to be an ensemble of actors; it would be playing in London; the *Complete Works* Festival would present every word that Shakespeare wrote.

The PACCAR Room in the transformed RST, named in recognition of a £1 million gift from the PACCAR Foundation

By 2005, with the bad headlines long gone and the RSC projecting a clear vision for its future, Arts Council England was ready to confirm its £50 million National Lottery grant (and went on to contribute an extra £3 million); it was the last major grant of its kind.

An approach to Advantage West Midlands, the regional development agency, brought in a promise of £20.4 million, not least because it recognised that the RSC was at that time worth £58 million a year to the regional economy. The agency could not however provide any money for The Courtyard because its rules stated that they could give nothing to anything temporary.

The next stage in the fundraising campaign was to seek major gifts from private donors. 'It was about making friends with people who were well disposed to the RSC,' said Graeme Williamson, Deputy Director of Development. 'You look for your nearest and dearest, the people who can make the really big gifts. Philanthropy in its purest form is about wanting to support something that is genuinely good. People who are close to us wanted to support the Transformation project because they felt it was right for the Company.'

The fundraising team and Heywood were careful to nurture donor friends, who in previous times might have received not much more than a polite thank you letter. Susie Sainsbury became the leader of the fundraising team, attending hundreds of events and eating countless suppers as she met and developed relationships with donors; some of whom, having given once, might be happy to give again or to suggest other possible supporters.

The Gatsby Charitable Foundation, established by Sainsbury's husband Lord Sainsbury in 1967, contributed £16 million. Other trusts were willing to show their support. The Garfield Weston Foundation, which has had a 20-year relationship with the RSC, gave £2 million, in recognition of which the new public open space (with spreading chestnut tree) in the shadow of the tower was named Weston Square. Similarly, the main new exhibition space inside the theatre is named the PACCAR Room to acknowledge a £1 million gift from Mark Pigott's PACCAR Foundation.

The Michigan-based Kresge Foundation made a gift of $1 million and so continued the long tradition of American support for theatre in Stratford: John D Rockefeller supported the building of the Shakespeare Memorial Theatre in 1932 with a cheque for $100,000, the largest gift of any donor, and his son David contributed the same sum to the Transformation fund; the creation of the Swan in 1986 was made possible because of funds donated by US philanthropist Frederick R Koch.

The fundraisers built on those long-established US connections. Susie Sainsbury became the non-voting Chair of RSC America, a formally constituted independent board from which the RSC could request funds but only for specific projects: RSC America supported the *Histories* cycle and also funded the 2011 residency in New York.

The Company also found a major donor closer to home. Research identified Elnora Ferguson as a regular at productions in the Swan. Detailed analysis then revealed her connection with the West Midlands-based Allan and Nesta Ferguson Charitable Trust, set up in memory of two generations of the Ferguson family to promote their particular interests in education, international friendship and understanding, and the promotion of world peace and development.

When approached by the RSC, Mrs Ferguson agreed to support the production of *Midnight's Children* in 2003 and later contributed £1.2 million to the Transformation project. Mrs Ferguson died suddenly in December 2008 and Miles Richardson, a member of the *Histories* ensemble, read at her funeral.

A number of the RSC's own actors helped with fund-raising from 2004. Once they realised they were not

Weston Square, named in recognition of the Garfield Weston Foundation's £2 million gift to the campaign

It proclaimed that, as the transformation of the RST neared completion, the Company was coming home. It was widely viewed and £10,000 was donated within two days of its launch.

David Tennant lends his support to the Take Your Seat appeal

→

Making the *We're Coming Home* film, which involved 160 costumed volunteers

being required to beg people for cash or pass round a hat, they were happy to turn up at informal functions to eat, drink and talk to donors who enjoyed chatting with King Lear or one of Cleopatra's attendants. Sir Patrick Stewart, who joined the RSC in 1966 and stayed for 12 years, said he had always looked on the Company as his theatrical home. 'Having acquired, as a result of my years in Hollywood, a certain reputation I could be of value to the Company and I was very happy for it to make as much use of me as possible. I wasn't being used. I was giving something back to an organisation that had given me everything.'

David Tennant also helped unlock purses and wallets. Jane Hains, who had seen his Hamlet five times, bought both a brick and a seat and contributed to another seat bought by the Tennant fan club. '*Hamlet* totally rekindled a love I had of Shakespeare that had been dormant for getting on for 30 years,' she told appeal organisers.

As the RSC's fundraisers continued their research and made friends with new donors, the Company published a three-minute film starring more than 160 costumed volunteers and alumni on its website and YouTube in spring 2010.

Others, meanwhile, were making individual efforts to raise cash. Board member David Burbidge led a highly successful campaign to raise money from local businesses and individuals. Sir Christopher Bland heroically decided to see every production in the *Complete Works* season and, a persuasive man, he drew up a formidable list of sponsors. 'I saw everything, even a rehearsed reading of *The Two Noble Kinsmen* on a wet Sunday afternoon in the Swan.' He raised £150,000 and heard every word Shakespeare wrote.

One September day in 2004, a new full-size auditorium was created backstage at the Royal Opera House, Covent Garden, for the Royal Shakespeare Company.

It had a thrust stage, three galleries, curtains for walls and an audience made up of helium-filled balloons. What the balloons made of the experience was not clear. But the exercise gave Michael Boyd and his RSC team their first chance to move away from computer screen impressions to see what their preferred auditorium would look like in the flesh. The team even brought in a cherry-picker so that they could dangle from on high to assess what the view would be like from the seats at the top.

The RSC had made considerable progress in defining the kind of auditorium it wanted

The shape of things to come: left, the Covent Garden experiment;

far left, Michael Boyd inspects a model of the RST's new auditorium at the offices of Bennetts Associates

in the reconstructed Royal Shakespeare Theatre even before Ian Ritchie began sketching the steel box that would become The Courtyard in his black notebook. Boyd and Flip Tanner, Technical Coordinator of the Transformation project, called in Anne Minors Performance Consultants to review their work. Minors carried out two studies, covering issues such as sightlines, acoustics, balcony design and the optimum number of seats, and her conclusions found their way into both the Covent Garden model and the design of The Courtyard Theatre's interior.

09

The Courtyard was made flesh by a conspiracy between the in-house team of Flip Tanner, Tom Piper [the RSC's Associate Designer], Charcoalblue and me, and then between all of us and Ian Ritchie Architects,' said Boyd.

'We were just very tough clients – we knew what we wanted and people came up with different ideas.'

Theatre consultancy Charcoalblue, founded by four young specialists in London in February 2004, has worked on projects that include the Young Vic, the Unicorn Theatre, the Roundhouse and Liverpool's Bluecoat Arts Centre. Its Managing Director, Andy Hayles, had already cast his eye over some of the schemes devised by Boyd and Tanner on their secret computer before the company was formally engaged by the RSC late in 2004. Hayles and Charcoalblue's Creative Director Jon Stevens were delighted, not least because both had Stratford links: Stevens was born in the town, went to Shakespeare's old school and was an assistant electrician at the Swan for three years; Hayles had spent a season as a follow-spot operator with the RSC.

Models for The Courtyard Theatre, one with two galleries, the other with three

Hayles thought the steel shed was an inspired idea but could see scope for improvements. Charcoalblue had initially been asked to look at the technical fit-out and audience accommodation in the temporary theatre and arranged a technical and an auditorium presentation to show what might be done.

The company's second presentation to the RSC took place in the kitchen of Vikki Heywood's home in north London. 'We presented a scheme for stalls and three balconies rather than two. They were sufficiently interested to get us to work up the scheme to see if it was worth taking further, which we did in January and February 2005. For a little while we were running two models. We then started one of the most enjoyable design processes I have ever been involved in. Tom Piper got his model makers to make models of both the two gallery and three gallery schemes and we went to the RSC rehearsal room to pace things out.

'We all decided and agreed that our three gallery scheme was not as good as the two gallery. We sat there with all the assembled RSC associates and everyone stuck their heads inside the model. Some

loved the three galleries, describing it as an epic space, like Old Trafford. But Greg Doran wondered how he could play comedy in it and how intimate quiet moments would be. The Colosseum in Rome is great for throwing Christians to the lions but an intimate two-hander play would not necessarily work so well there.'

Hayles discovered that although the RSC was very familiar with the 430-seat Swan, it had no experience of how to lay out seats in a large courtyard space. 'An awful lot of people were convinced it would not work. They said you could not create an open stage with a thousand seats round it without running into huge difficulties – some cited the case of the Olivier at the National Theatre. But Michael Boyd suggested that the Crucible in Sheffield, where he had been Artistic Director in the 1980s, was a more encouraging precedent.'

Hayles and his team asked themselves many questions: how wide should the stage be? What should be the relationship between the stage and the front row? And the back row? How should you seat the audience – in little communities or in one big sweep? 'The theatre design mantra says that you design from the inside out. The fact that we already had a rusty box enclosure fought against that. But we were going fast and decided not to worry. We had our four walls so we worked out towards them.'

The Courtyard Theatre went through 27 versions before reaching its final form and Hayles suggests there were some spirited skirmishes with Ian Ritchie along the way. 'But he was fabulous at driving the scheme on. There are not many architects who would put their reputations on the line for a scheme like that.'

This prompts questions about where the work of an architect stops and that of a theatre consultant begins. 'Ian Ritchie was a tough customer, with very strong ideas

Proscenium arch versus thrust stage: different shapes, different seat colours in the old RST and The Courtyard

about the space,' said Piper. 'He wanted to get involved with the auditorium and some of the interior finishes and for a long time he wanted blue seats rather than red.'

In the book on The Courtyard published by Ian Ritchie Architects, Ritchie writes: 'A deep blue was considered too cold and "blood" from performances needs to "vanish" into a red carpet.' Swayed by this practical necessity to mop up the spilled gore from Shakespeare's more violent moments; by Boyd's romantic attachment to the scarlet auditoriums created for Victorian and Edwardian theatres by Frank Matcham; and by the sensuous colour of a ripe plum, Ritchie appears to have seen the red light. When The Courtyard opened in June 2006, he told *The Guardian*: 'Mauves and purples, as in the old Royal Shakespeare Theatre, are for convention centres. Red is for theatres.'

Piper said that he and others involved in the design feared that The Courtyard (and also the new RST) could end up looking like a scaled-up Swan. 'We were trying to find a space that could be both epic and intimate – unlike the Swan. For a time a lot of decisions were about how we could make The Courtyard look less like the Swan. So we thought we should have chrome mesh instead of railings at the front of the galleries. I remember being with Michael in the Swan and holding up bits of mesh. There were a lot of battles. But in the end we found mesh didn't give that sense of enclosure that railings do.'

Steel railings also helped with sightlines when actors moved to the edge of the stage. It was Piper's idea that the ends of the galleries should be angled towards the stage as another strategy in the plan to bind audience and actor together. 'That was where architecture and theatre practice didn't quite click,' he said. 'I was intrigued by the design process. It was much more confrontational than it would later be with the RST. But on the other hand it was more creative in a funny kind of way because it was that much faster.'

There were inevitably some niggles. 'The problem we found almost at once was the acoustic in the back row of the stalls,' said Andy Hayles. 'That was a complete surprise to everyone. You could sit in the back seat of the second gallery and hear perfectly, even if the actor was talking with his back to the audience. But the back row of the stalls was a challenge, although the row in front was just about OK. The acoustic explanation for all this was extremely complex. The RSC took a row of seats off and deployed them elsewhere. This problem generated a lot of thinking about what are the good seats in a theatre: is it a good seat if you can hear? Or if you can see?'

Once The Courtyard Theatre opened, a much more worrying problem loomed: people were not coming and tickets were not selling. Perhaps, despite all the huge hoardings round the RST proclaiming that the Company was still in business, some thought the RSC had closed down while rebuilding went ahead; perhaps, despite excellent reviews, others didn't fancy a cycle of history plays.

Whatever the reason, the slump in ticket sales caused anxiety at the top of the RSC. 'It was scary,' said Heywood. 'So we approached Central Television and did a free ticket scheme with them to get people to come and experience The Courtyard. That moment of inspiration got us over that hump of audience resistance.

'We gave away a huge number of tickets. It was incredibly important that The Courtyard opened on time, filled up with people and that those people liked it. If we hadn't got The Courtyard open on time and on budget, I think we would have lost an enormous amount of support for the scheme to reconstruct the RST and the entire credibility of the organisation would have been threatened. If the first thing we did went wrong, then people would say we couldn't even build a temporary theatre in a car park.'

→ Supporting act: a blue steel frame holds up the front wall of the RST. Hoardings point audiences towards The Courtyard

Boyd's eight-play *Histories* cycle (*The Guardian's* 'production of the decade') emphatically showed what this new theatre could do as actors defied vertigo to descend from ladders, bridges and ropes to launch into eye-filling action that contrasted with moments of intense intimacy. 'Boyd makes brilliant use of The Courtyard, in that he directs vertically and thinks laterally,' wrote Michael Billington in *The Guardian*.

The Independent's Paul Taylor agreed: 'The vertiginous instability of a political world where everyone is fighting on two fronts (with the French and with one another) is superbly evoked. This is not to be missed.'

3-D Shakespeare:
Henry VI, Part I in
The Courtyard

Courtyard tragedies:
David Tennant as Hamlet,
Sir Ian McKellen as
King Lear

A full house at
The Courtyard Theatre

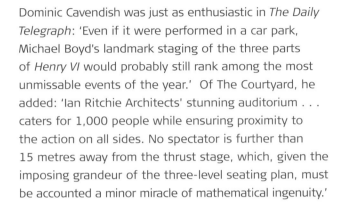

Dominic Cavendish was just as enthusiastic in *The Daily Telegraph*: 'Even if it were performed in a car park, Michael Boyd's landmark staging of the three parts of *Henry VI* would probably still rank among the most unmissable events of the year.' Of The Courtyard, he added: 'Ian Ritchie Architects' stunning auditorium . . . caters for 1,000 people while ensuring proximity to the action on all sides. No spectator is further than 15 metres away from the thrust stage, which, given the imposing grandeur of the three-level seating plan, must be accounted a minor miracle of mathematical ingenuity.'

Ticket sales soon boomed and continued well, helped by Gregory Doran's *Hamlet* for our time with David Tennant as the prince and Sir Ian McKellen's long-awaited Lear in a production by Sir Trevor Nunn. Later would come Michael Boyd's *As You Like It* ('intelligent, deeply felt, admirably spoken,' *Daily Telegraph*) and Rupert Goold's *Romeo and Juliet*, the most exciting revival since Zeffirelli, as far as Michael Billington could recall.

The Board could now begin to take stock of what had been achieved. 'It's not often that architects exceed expectations – if only because most clients' hopes are often unreasonably high,' said Sir Christopher Bland. 'Our hopes were exactly that –

and we got more, and better, than we bargained for, on time and on budget.

'Watching the first public performance from the furthest seat was proof that we had achieved our aims for our audience, in a splendid and charismatic setting.'

The decision to opt for a thrust stage was based on Boyd's certainty that it was the right theatre form for Shakespeare and for the RSC. 'Once we had committed

to a thrust stage in The Courtyard, we were then committed to a thrust stage in the new RST,' added Bland. 'We were persuaded because we had spent some time analysing whether anywhere in the world there was a successful combination of thrust and proscenium and had come to the conclusion that there was not.

'That in a sense forced our hand, but it was a direction in which we were happy to go. If The Courtyard had not worked, if everyone had said this was a thrust too far, we could still have influenced the design for the RST.'

Whether that switch would have been quite so easy is open to debate. But in the end, it did not matter:

for many, The Courtyard Theatre was a vindication of the case for the thrust stage.

Ritchie went to see dozens of performances in the theatre and concluded that it had been 'fantastically successful'. In *The Guardian*, James Fenton wrote of seeing *Richard III* in the new theatre and said what many were already feeling: 'Nobody who has seen [The Courtyard] supposes for a moment that it will be pulled down in the near future.'

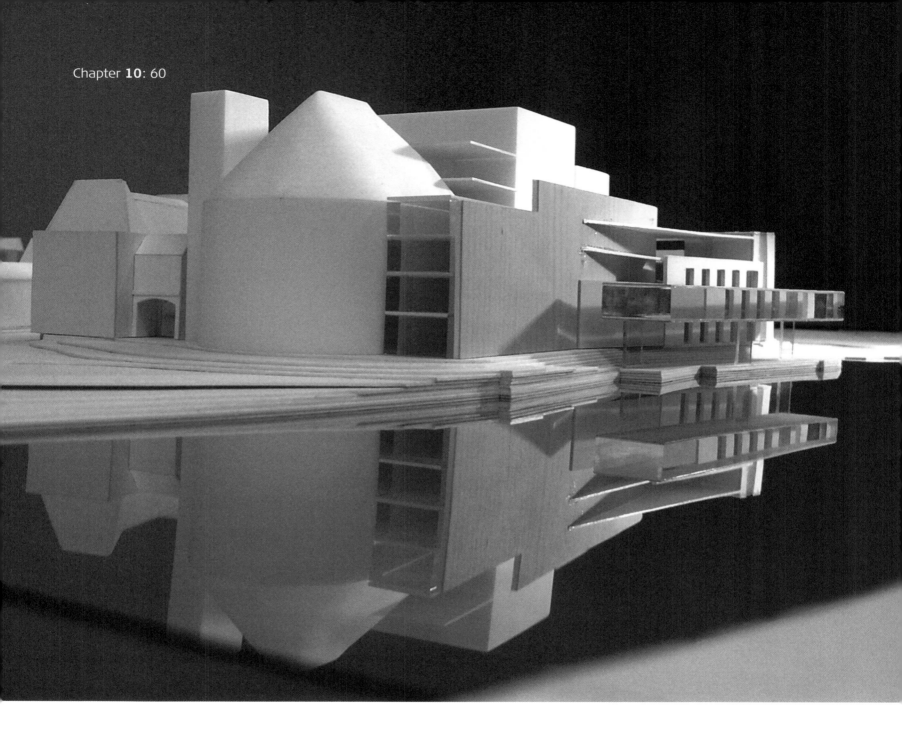

An early Bennetts Associates'
model, showing an initial plan
for the riverside façade

In 2003 Bennetts Associates, an architectural practice based in a former barn and printworks in Islington, north London, completed the new Hampstead Theatre.

It was the first time the practice, founded by Rab Bennetts and his wife Denise in 1987, had designed a theatre and members of the design team had enjoyed their time on stage.

So they took note when, in 2004, the RSC advertised the contract to transform the Royal Shakespeare Theatre. The project was discussed in the practice's elegant offices, with their mix of steel, glass and bare brick, a couple of minutes from the Angel and Upper Street. In the end, the directors decided not to submit an application. 'We thought the RSC would go for the glitterati and that we would have no chance of winning the job,' said Rab Bennetts.

Simon Erridge (left) and Rab Bennetts of Bennetts Associates

'We decided it would probably go to one of the world's star architects and it wasn't worth even applying

because these big international competitions are always a stitch-up. Or they go to a certain type of architect and we are a bit too modest for that.'

The day before applications closed Ian Ritchie, an RSC governor and architect of The Courtyard Theatre's steel shed, called to check that Bennetts had thrown their architectural hat into the ring. 'You really must,' he said. So they did. But they left it rather late. 'We decided to do the submission 12 hours before the deadline. It was the quickest one we have ever done,' said Simon Erridge, the director who was eventually to lead the RST project for Bennetts.

After the previous plan, which might or might not have led to the demolition of the RST, members of the RSC's Board and senior staff had carefully considered the kind of architect they were seeking for a new scheme. 'For several years the RSC had lived with a particular kind of architect in Erick van Egeraat and was alert to the issues that had arisen out of that relationship,' said Michael Boyd. 'The Company was keen to improve its relationship with an architect, to find one the RSC would find it easy to become intimate with.'

Boyd himself did not feel daunted by the pressure to search out the right firm for the job. 'Other people more involved in the earlier process might have been more daunted than I was.'

They were. 'We were looking for someone who would work collaboratively from the very beginning and would enjoy the kind of shared experience we were having with Ian Ritchie on The Courtyard,' said Susie Sainsbury, Deputy Chair of the RSC and Chair of the Board's Transformation project committee.

Vikki Heywood, who had only just taken up her post as the RSC's Executive Director when the hunt for an architect began, was very aware of the need to get it right and Sir Christopher Bland, the equally new Chairman of the RSC, had a clear vision of the architect the Company needed. 'We were looking for somebody who could bring some imagination to what could have been a very restrictive and constrained project,' said Bland.

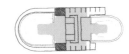
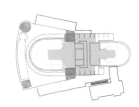

Bennetts Associates' initial concept plans for the RST, developed around the immovable fly tower

'It could have been regarded as a plan simply to gut and replace the inside of the RST. We wanted something better than that and more imaginative. We also needed someone with experience of what happens in theatres.'

Enter Bennetts, with their experience of the new Hampstead Theatre. Rab Bennetts admits he was gobsmacked when his practice made it on to a shortlist of eight. He and Erridge had by this stage taken themselves off to Stratford to see the theatre and see a play. Bennetts had never been a fan of Shakespeare at school; Erridge made his first visit to the RST as a student when he saw *As You Like It* from a seat in the back row of the balcony. He never went back. Neither had seen a thrust stage until they went to the Swan.

All eight practices were interviewed by the RSC's selection panel. 'Our interview went brilliantly,' said Bennetts. 'It was one of those days when we were on a high. We enjoyed the whole thing, got on with everyone. It was fantastic. And so we got on to a shortlist of three.'

Bennetts were competing with O'Donnell and Tuomey of Dublin (whose work includes an art gallery at University College Cork) and MacCormac Jamieson Pritchard (now MJP Architects) of London, who designed the elegant Ruskin Library at Lancaster University. Each of the three contenders was asked to make a presentation in their own office and then attend a final interview.

'There are very few clients who take the trouble to go and visit the architects in their own offices, see some buildings they have done and take up references,' said Rab Bennetts.

When the RSC team went to Islington, they were taken into a meeting room whose rough exposed beams revealed that it had once formed part of the barn. The Bennetts Associates team, which now included Project Architect

Alasdair McKenzie, arrived at the presentation armed with a cardboard box and proceeded to think out of that box with the help of bits of polystyrene, key props in their version of a theatrical transformation scene. They started with a drawing of the whole of the river area that ran the entire length of a completely blank table. As they talked through the scheme, gradually adding polystyrene blocks, it became blindingly obvious that they were taking a view that went way beyond the RST. 'We started with the existing building, took bits away and added bits,' said Erridge.

'We ended up with a complete concept as a model sitting in its context, all generated out of a cardboard box.'

This was a workshop, not a presentation of a finished scheme: Bennetts were actively involving the RSC team in the design of their new theatre. 'That's how we work,' said Bennetts. 'There's an idea among the public that the architect comes in with a fully formed idea and presents it. The reality for us is a partnership. The idea is to orchestrate the process rather than monopolise it. But we don't pretend we have all the answers.'

Bennetts were going out of their way to prove that they were collaborators, a quality they knew the RSC valued and wanted. 'We find on the whole that we get on with people and like working with people for a long period of time,' added Rab Bennetts. 'If you want a prima donna to come along, put something on the table and say, "That's how you are going to do it", that's not really our bag at all. We need to bounce ideas off clients and I think the RSC felt we were people they could work with.'

Heywood initially found it strange to work on such a major project as part of a group of argumentative and opinionated individuals who had ultimately to operate by consensus (she called it a 'multi-headed beast';

An early concept drawing prepared for the architectural competition showing the RSC sites in red

Rab Bennetts referred to the project team as the Gang of Five: Vikki Heywood, Susie Sainsbury, Michael Boyd, Sir Christopher Bland and Peter Wilson). During the reconstruction of the Royal Court, she had been in sole command of delivering the project, an experience she had found 'unbelievably frightening and lonely'.

'Reaching consensus is a daily difficulty but it's one I would always rather have. We had wrangles, furies and frustrations on a daily basis but at least I was not sitting at home alone thinking "I am the only person who knows everything. I am the only person who is going to be able to solve all these problems and I don't know what we are going to start on tomorrow".'

A key part of the RST scheme emerged from the Bennetts box. Rab Bennetts and Erridge had placed a dumpy polystyrene block between the old balcony entrance and Waterside, suggesting it could be some kind of pavilion to contain what was emerging as a new public square. Bennetts suggests that either he or Erridge then turned the block on its end. Boyd also had a hand in this significant action and remembers the polystyrene block as being the size of a cigarette packet.

A tower was born. The RSC had not asked for one and it was not in the original brief. But Bennetts and Erridge realised that the new structure would be a dramatic addition to the scheme. 'Michael used the word breakthrough at that point, which was a very positive thing to say when we were still at the interview stage,' said Bennetts. 'It looked as if we had actually got something that would lift the spirit. And the Victorian theatre had once had a tower until it burnt down.'

'That session with the box of tricks was fun,' said Heywood. 'Rab and Simon listened and changed things as people were talking. We started to design the building in that session. That convinced me that we were

Fire sweeps the Memorial Theatre in 1926

An early tower concept model (above); later development models of the tower brickwork (below)

already on the journey. So why not keep going with the people who were really beginning to crack some of the problems?'

Bennetts Associates got the job, not least because they knew how to laugh. 'They giggled,' said Heywood. 'They looked as if they would be good gigglers, which is all part of it. They were prepared to roll up their sleeves and play. I am not saying they are without ego – no architect in the land is – but they have the ability to subvert their ego for the audience they are with. That's really good. They also fundamentally understood the concept of on time and on budget. Some architects don't, particularly architects who are attracted to high-profile artistic projects.'

Bland describes Bennetts as pragmatic. 'They can be stubborn and difficult – but then most good creative people are.'

The official announcement of the appointment of Bennetts Associates was made on 18 March 2005, a week after Stratford-on-Avon District Council granted planning permission for The Courtyard. Boyd commented that the RSC had found the right people 'to join us in creating a

more intimate space that our house playwright would recognise as a theatre'. Rab Bennetts told *The Guardian*: 'We are not daunted. The question still to be answered is to what degree the theatre is going to be altered and I don't think we will necessarily end up ripping it apart. It is a picturesque building but it is not in good shape.'

Before Bennetts could start drawing up detailed plans, they had to discover whether what the RSC wanted – a new thrust stage auditorium constructed between the Art Deco foyer and the immovable fly tower – was possible. They launched a feasibility study to examine whether Boyd's certainty, based on those covert investigations on his computer, was justified. By October, the study had established that the new auditorium would fit, although it would be a tight squeeze, and the only reason it would fit was because the interior walls of the old auditorium could, thanks to the dispensation from English Heritage, be demolished.

Bennetts were fully aware of the constraints facing them but still preferred the challenge of the existing RST to a greenfield site. 'If you are doing an existing building where you can take the roof off and hollow out the middle, the constraints are so great that they force you to invention,' said Rab Bennetts. 'In theatre particularly, the discovery of an existing item in a found space is part of the life of theatre. Theatre people have always revelled in that kind of thing. So an existing building, cut and carved, is perfect for them.'

Heywood agrees with Bennetts' assessment of theatre people. 'I have never done anything that did not have a constraint to it,' she said. 'I just wouldn't know how to function if someone offered me a great big empty field and asked what I would like the new building to look like. I like constraint because that is where the challenge is

and that's where the ghosts are.'

Box of tricks: the model prepared for the architectural competition

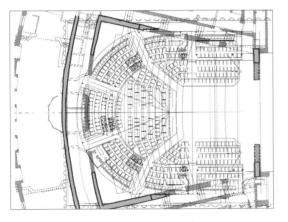

An early plan showing the new auditorium overlaid on the existing walls of the RST

to the reality of what at first was a £45 million budget for the RST.' Heywood was also keen to make sure that members of the Company realised that the new building would not fulfil their wildest dreams. 'One of the problems with a Company like this is that it has an enormous amount of aspiration and ambition and a desire to want to improve anything and everything. So it wanted every pound to make ten pounds' worth of difference and that was never going to happen. It wanted this project to resolve all the problems it had ever had since it was founded, which it was never going to do.'

Peter Wilson, the former Project Director for both Tate Modern and the Tate Britain Centenary Development, had been appointed Director of the Transformation project in January 2005: whenever he was asked how a scheme could be delivered on time and on budget, he would always reply: 'You need enough time and a big enough budget.' He was well aware that artistic ambitions could run riot and his job was to deal with people, their disappointments and their aspirations. 'In any arts organisation, and this is no different from how it was at the Tate, there are boundless ambitions and sometimes conflicting ambitions. Arts organisations jog along for years on quite small budgets and suddenly find they have millions of pounds to spend in a few years. Everyone is bound to start to think that that is a huge sum of money, that they can have everything they want.

Members of both the Transformation project team and the RSC Board were aware that they would have to manage the expectations of the Company's staff. 'In all arts projects, there is a tendency to theorise about an endless list of perfect scenarios,' said Bennetts. 'But they can't have it; in an existing building you have to have some restraint.'

'One of the biggest problems early on was managing the expectations of departments who all thought they were going to get the Royal Opera House [which reopened in 1999 after a three-year, £214 million renovation scheme],' added Erridge. 'We had to bring that down

'You have to start explaining to people the 80% rule: it's best to get something that is nearly what you wanted than to hold out for 100% and never be satisfied. Some people find that quite difficult, particularly people with a creative bent – they find it difficult to sign up to anything other than perfection. It's not that they don't understand imperfection but their goal is perfection, for which they are always striving. Project directors don't do that. They say, "Here's the best we can get. That's the goal". Perfection is a balanced set of imperfections.'

As they sharpened their pencils and began the design process the Bennetts team, which was to grow to 16 architects at the peak of the project, was well aware that the RSC was not looking for a shimmering culture palace but a reborn Royal Shakespeare Theatre that would honour the oft-mentioned ghosts in its walls:

the old RST might have been a long way from perfect but it had seen some great performances in its 75 years.

A cast iron spiral staircase from the 1932 building, retained backstage in the new RST

Michael Boyd embraced an aesthetic labelled as shabby chic, a concept best defined as an aura of creative tattiness (with perhaps a whiff of sweat and old make-up); one that stimulates the theatrical imagination rather more than spotless newness. Boyd had worked with the RSC's Associate Designer Tom Piper at the Tron Theatre in Glasgow, an old church that they bashed about a bit when they staged *Macbeth*. Piper had also worked on the conversion of Peter Brook's famously and effectively tatty Théâtre des Bouffes du Nord in Paris.

'All theatre people seem to prefer the character and excitement of a found space like the Tramway in Glasgow

A concept sketch of the new square on Waterside

[a former tram shed] and the surprise successes like the Young Vic [a former butcher's shop],' said Piper. 'One of the things we always felt about the RST was that there was a preciousness in it that you couldn't mess around with or destroy. The challenge for me was how to create a permanent theatre space that had that atmosphere,

that feeling of found environment, a space people wouldn't feel afraid to mess about.'

Piper and others on the project team had confidence that Bennetts Associates would find the right solution; after all, the practice's own offices were a fusion of the historic (their converted barn was where cattle were kept before the final leg of the journey to Smithfield market) and the new.

Bennetts and Erridge knew that Boyd and others had very firm ideas on the kind of auditorium they wanted, ideas that had germinated over several years and were being tested at The Courtyard. 'It would have been the height of arrogance to suggest that we had better ideas for the auditorium,' said Bennetts. 'We took the view that the auditorium was a hugely significant but small part of a much bigger project.'

Old and new: the theatre's riverside façade

As their workshop with the RSC had shown, they were looking beyond the walls of the RST to what Bennetts calls the Company's campus, and to the town. 'The creation of squares, routes, public spaces and a new landmark [the tower] meant that this was as much about the public realm as it was about a new auditorium for the performance of Shakespeare.'

Bennetts became very attached to the idea of engagement: actors engage with the audience; the Company has to engage with the town; the building has to engage with its setting. If the old jam-factory RST ever looked outwards towards the town, it did so through small windows on the grim Waterside wall.

Bennetts and his team decided that wall would, with the addition of a double-height glazed colonnade, become a new main entrance that would for the first time connect the RST and the Swan and contain both box office and shop. The new tower would point the way and look over a new public square, a threshold, a place for pre-play mingling and for performance. It would also, wrote Bennetts in notes on his bid for the RST contract, be a focal point for the Company's many routes and connections, 'an external "hallway" between

the administration, workshops, education rooms, get-in, rehearsal spaces and dressing rooms . . .

It could become analogous to the courtyard of a Renaissance institution.'

Bennetts likes his Shakespearean connections: in the same notes, he labelled the Waterside and Avon frontages as respectively 'urban' and 'rural' and added: 'Shakespeare often writes about court and country, about the aristocracy of noble houses and the ordinary lives of those on the outside. Is there a connection here? Could the external walls of the reworked theatre invoke the same sense of contrast?'

Something certainly had to be done about the messy rural (or Avon) side to restore it to something close to Elisabeth Scott's original vision. It was no longer a 'sweet and lovely wall': various accretions, including the balcony café (added in 1936), the restaurant and terrace café (1938) and the dressing rooms and green room (1950-51) would have to go. Windows and some sadly bashed about brickwork would be restored; a new four-storey block of dressing rooms would be added, plus a new stage door building; and the entire sweep would regain its former elegance.

Bennetts also wanted to transform the pedestrian riverside route past the RST and Swan. It used to begin secretively by the exterior wall of the fountain court and staircase, continue narrowly past the terrace café and then twist below the green room from which posing actors (rude mechanicals taking tea or soldiers having a quick cigarette before death at Agincourt) could look down on passing punters. The path eventually staggered out into the gardens behind the Swan. Bennetts decided they would create a new wider, fully-accessible and far less apologetic walkway running past the theatres, through the gardens and on via a new section that

The new riverside walkway

Sketch of the space between the 1932 foyer and the drum wall

would cut out the steps at the chain ferry and continue through a new gate in the churchyard wall to end at Holy Trinity. If nothing else, the path would be a splendid approach for a wedding party.

The team had to retain the listed canopy over what had been the main entrance but decided to remove the glazed enclosure added in 1958. This façade would also be restored, with a clean-up for the five panels by sculptor Eric Kennington (Treachery, Jollity, Martial Ardour, Love, and Life Triumphing Over Death) above.

Inside, the Art Deco foyer, the circle bar above it and the fountain court and staircase would be restored to their former glory to provide new café and bar spaces, and the new auditorium would be enclosed by a brick-faced concrete drum. 'Between the back of the auditorium and the back of the Art Deco rooms is a residual space that should encapsulate the frisson between old and new,' Rab Bennetts wrote in English Heritage's conservation bulletin. 'Constricted but lofty, it will be full of glimpses between the foyers and the auditorium that should enrich the experience of arrival and departure.'

It would also enrich the experience of hanging about, reading the programme and watching other people; there was never much space for creative lurking in the old RST.

But with the move of staff out of the building into a new suite of offices attached to the back of the Union Club on Chapel Lane, Bennetts had much more space to play with. The new RST would be an open and welcoming building, through which playgoers and visitors could move easily from main entrance to the river and to the upper levels.

Bennetts' significant innovation would be the 36-metre tower with an observation platform giving panoramic views over the town, the Vale of Evesham and the memory of Shakespeare's own Forest of Arden; it would shout to visitors and residents alike of the presence of the Royal Shakespeare Company. 'We were changing the geometry of a ruthlessly symmetrical building and creating a new focus to one side of it,' said Erridge. 'It needed a marker, something to identify it.

He and Bennetts were both remembering the tower that had graced the original Memorial Theatre: until it was reduced to a stump after the 1926 fire, it had complemented the graceful spire of Holy Trinity, where Shakespeare was baptised and buried. The proposed new tower was not going to turn Stratford into Warwickshire's San Gimignano but it was a bold, and as it turned out, controversial part of the scheme: some

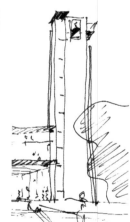

Above left: the original Memorial Theatre, with tower;

above, sketch of the new tower by Rab Bennetts

Stratford residents were less than convinced by this proposed intrusion on the town's skyline; Sir Christopher Bland, Chairman of the RSC, was concerned about the cost.

The tower was the clearest example of how Bennetts were thinking beyond the walls of the theatre to its context, its setting on its much-loved riverside site. 'Shakespeare frequently refers to Italy, where family castles often express themselves through towers,' said Erridge, who had caught Bennetts' affection for Shakespearean influences.

'It seemed quite an appropriate metaphor – and it would also give great views.'

He had Lucca, the medieval city in northern Tuscany, in mind and the proposed colonnade would have more than a whiff of Bologna; Shakespeare himself had referred to 'yonder tower' where some were wont 'to overpeer the city' in *Henry VI, Part I*.

As Bennetts struggled to get the tower right, experts from the RSC's own design team went to Islington to help make 20 or so models, some of which still sit on shelves in the architects' office. Architects usually make their models from inscrutable white card; the RSC team came up with the idea of making the models with a brick effect to achieve a more realistic view of its scale and finish.

Bennetts wanted the tower to look almost as if it was part of Scott's design for the 1932 theatre that had never been built, but the need to install two lifts in the tower was a major barrier to a pleasing design. Eventually one of those lifts was moved into the theatre because it needed only to serve as far as the rooftop restaurant. With a single lift the tower became much simpler, much thinner, much purer in its geometry.

Its shape was modified following discussions at the Stratford-on-Avon District Council meeting when the

whole RST scheme won planning permission. 'Originally it had a different shape to the walls, a slightly different cantilever to the topmost balcony,' said Bennetts. 'It was asymmetrical and twisted. At the planning permission meeting, two committee members said they liked everything about the project but just didn't like the tower. I said to them in the chamber, after the project was approved, that I was prepared to have another look.

'I did more drawings and came up with the idea of the octagon that changes over its height into a square.

'We twigged that the fountain staircase in the Art Deco foyer was an incomplete 16-sided figure and that the new auditorium was based on a 12-sided figure. So we wondered if an eight-sided figure would suit the tower. If you start off with an octagon and it reduces in thickness towards the top and becomes a square, then the sides all become geometrical shapes which all look interesting from a distance.'

Beyond aesthetic consideration, those interestingly-shaped sides, with their extremely complex brickwork, had a crucial function: they would hold the tower up.

An octagon that changes over its height into a square: the RSC's new tower

INTERVAL 02

Somewhere on the riverside wall of the Royal Shakespeare Theatre is a brick with the name 'Nigel Page' inscribed on the interior face. It would be impossible to number the bricks laid by Page during his year on the site but that signature was his very modest sign of the pride he took in the job.

Page, who lives in Birmingham, is self-employed and was recommended to brickwork contractors Lesterose. 'The first thing I thought was, "Great – a year's work". I didn't know a lot about it, to be honest. I'd never been to Stratford, even though it's only 30 miles away.'

Most of his work was on refurbishing brickwork. 'I was doing a lot of chopping-out, trying to save the good bricks and getting rid of the rubbish ones. They gave me a book of the remedial work that was needed and just said basically, "Go to it". It was a great job because there was so much to do and I had a free rein at it. I did 90 per cent of the work on the riverside wall, where I had to take sections out that were broken or cracked.

'I'd save the good bricks, mix them with the new handmade bricks and then try to put them in so that they didn't stand out like a sore thumb. It was a repair but they didn't want it either to look too new or to blend so much that you would never know it was there. That was quite a hard effect to get.'

Page also set coping stones for the interior drum wall, worked on the new tower and renovated a range of freestanding arches, part of the 1932 Memorial Theatre façade, that had been left stranded in the restaurant when the roof was raised. 'The arches were in a right state when I started on them; they were literally falling down. We had the new brickwork tinted so that it all matched. I think it looks smart. That was a good little project.'

Repairs were also needed on the remains of the old tower of the Swan but it was impossible to rig up scaffolding there. So Page was hoisted up in a cage dangling from the jib of the huge tower crane. 'The first time I went up, my legs went funny. You'd take up your bricks and mortar and radio to the driver, "Down, left, right". Everyone on the site used to be looking at me up there. And then the driver would swing me out over the park and all the kids would be pointing at me.'

Page hopes some day to take his grandchildren to Stratford, show them a wall or two and say: 'I did that.' He added: 'At first, it was just another job. But now it's something I can tell people about because everyone has heard of the theatre. If I go to price a job up now, I can say, "I was a bricklayer on the RST". That's the way I look at it. It's a kind of a bragging thing.'

One late autumn day in 2008, ochre-coloured roof trusses, each 30 metres long and weighing 30 tonnes, were lowered by huge cranes on to the top of the new Royal Shakespeare Theatre. They slipped easily into place, anchored at each end by four bolts.

Juneann Hartley, a freelance site engineer hired by John Doyle Construction, had had the job of marking in advance where those bolts should go. Had she made a mistake, the trusses could not have been secured; time and much money would have been wasted. 'I remember distinctly marking out the holes for the bolts. Another engineer took the marks that I had put down and drilled the holes. Everything was fine; I had done this kind of thing before. There was nothing that gave me sleepless nights.'

But she had never worked on a theatre and was very enthusiastic about the job. 'I loved the idea of creating something new within the building's existing footprint, especially when I saw the Art Deco foyer and staircase and realised how they were marrying them with the new parts of this really exciting building. I'm a bit of an Art Deco fan. I like the look, I like the era and I like the films that came out at that time. I thought the whole thing was so worth preserving.'

Her work for the RSC required the same confident skills she had used on Birmingham's Bullring and other major projects. 'My job is to be the person on a site who is responsible for making sure that things are in exactly the right place. I help put on the ground the design shown on the plans.'

Hartley arrived in Stratford in April 2008 and stayed until Christmas. She worked on the understage basement, setting out the concrete caps that tied the piles together and then the concrete floor slabs. She moved on to the reinforced concrete wall at the back of the auditorium and after that to the theatre's summit to prepare for the arrival of those mighty roof trusses.

'The work was intensive but the people were terrific. If you are a woman on the site, all the men want to know is whether you can do the job. They ask, "Will she get the marks done before I get there? Will I be hanging around? Will she be wasting my time?" That's all they are interested in. And once I had proved myself, the banter was terrific. I'm proud of my part in the project. There was such a buzz and pride in the work that was going on.'

David Gilks worked on the reconstruction of the Royal Shakespeare Theatre, at first tidying up and checking for safety hazards and later operating the first lift (goods only at first) to enter service. 'No passengers were allowed. I had to turn RSC people away. I had a few snide remarks but I'm thick-skinned. I just said no.'

Gilks had attended Shakespeare's old school in Stratford and remembers visits to the theatre, especially a production of *Peter Pan*. He spent 40 years in the building trade until he entered a dark period in his life from which the RST helped save him.

He had a drink problem, lost his driving licence and late in 2009 moved out of his home to protect his family from eviction. He then slept rough by the chain ferry, near The Courtyard and in the shadow of the giant cranes working on the RST. 'There's a retaining wall and I just popped in under the bushes. It was a lovely little place. I was there for about five months. I survived.'

He eventually found a home in Alcester through Stonham Supported Housing, part of the Home Group, a national housing association. He wanted a job and to return to the building trade but couldn't get one without a Construction Skills Certification Scheme card, a certificate of basic health and safety competence.

To get the card, he would have to travel to Coventry to take a test. But he had no money for the fee or the bus fare. So Stonham's Caroline Snow applied to the Vicar's Relief Fund, part of the St Martin-in-the-Fields Christmas Charity Appeal, which makes small payments 'to help those who are in need or suffering hardship'. The fund contributed just over £60, enough to enable Gilks to catch the bus to Coventry, pass his test and pick up the crucial card. An agency put him in touch with Elliott Thomas, a construction logistics company involved in the Transformation project, and he started work on the RST site on 6 October 2009.

'To get work is a relief; it's a weight off your mind. I did general tidying up, making sure the guys on site were not going to trip over or fall down a hole. It wasn't mind-taxing but I had to see problems that might be caused by a lump of wood or trailing wire. I was also hoovering everywhere. Most of the building was hoover-only. Which was fair enough, because if you use a brush, you are only moving the dust somewhere else.

'I used to walk in from Alcester till I got an old bike, which had no brakes or gears. Then Caroline got me a new one from Halfords and I was leaving home at 4.50am to start on the site at 6am. When the weather was bad I hitchhiked to work.'

Even before construction work was complete, Gilks was promising himself he would be back to see a play in the new auditorium. He also defended the controversial tower, which he had helped clean. 'It's not an eyesore. You want to get up there. You can see the Welsh hills from the top.'

Bennetts' tower divided opinion in Stratford and beyond, but that controversy was a mere local spat compared with the row stirred up by the proposal, announced in March 2001, that the Royal Shakespeare Theatre should be demolished and replaced by a new building designed by Erick van Egeraat.

Dissenters organised themselves into HOOT (Hands Off Our Theatre). 'The plan was like a red rag to a bull to a number of people,' said HOOT founder member James Philpotts. 'About 12 of us got together and HOOT was formed to publicise the case against demolition.'

In January 2002, HOOT member and Stratford Town Councillor Michael Crutchley submitted a memorandum to the House of Commons Select Committee on Culture, Media and Sport, which was then considering the RSC's application for Lottery money towards the cost of the scheme.

In a powerful salvo, he complained that the Company was keeping Stratford in the dark.

He also insisted that the RST was 'part of the national and local heritage and to assist its destruction using public money appears to me to be manifestly wrong . . . There appears to be a crass attempt to foist the values of the few on the many . . . To ignore public opinion on such seemingly radical proposals is . . . in defiance of the rights of the people of Stratford-upon-Avon.'

Roger Mortlock, the RSC's former Director of Communications, leads a consultation event in the RST

1.2

'HOOT members demonstrated outside the theatre on a press night with someone dressed as a bear,' said Roger Mortlock, then the RSC's Director of Communications. 'We went and offered them tea. That was the moment we got into our stride rather than be defensive. We knew that lots of people in the town thought very different things about the theatre.'

(Philpotts has no memory of a bear, only of a supporter who would take to Stratford's streets in Elizabethan dress as 3,500 signatures were gathered for a petition.)

HOOT members told anyone who would listen that they understood the RSC's problem but claimed the Company (whose initial reaction to protests Philpotts described as 'contemptuous') had come up with the wrong solution.

When the demolition scheme was abandoned, the new senior members of the Company began to realise that meaningful consultation – and not just with HOOT – would be essential if any new plan was to succeed. Noble's reforms of the RSC had led to a concentration of staff in Stratford, with the (possibly unintended) consequence of making the RSC seem less remote and aloof in Shakespeare's home town. 'An organisation that had mostly looked down the M40 to London shifted to an organisation that realised it needed more of a dialogue-based relationship with Stratford,' said Mortlock.

When Vikki Heywood arrived as Executive Director in 2003, she soon decided that the RSC and Stratford had, as she put it, 'to get on'. She and other members of staff began meeting district and county councillors, and joined committees that were nothing to do with the RSC and its ambitions. 'When we went on to those committees, people began to perceive us as the puppet masters behind everything. But the RSC cannot sit here and not care about what the town is like, not become engaged at a local level. So we began to get engaged.

Some of that was driven entirely selfishly and some by a desire to behave appropriately. Our relationship with the town is complicated, but strong.'

Local people were being invited into a conversation with the RSC; that hadn't happened before. Boyd also decided that the RSC had to have a 'robust, heartfelt and well thought-out programme' for communicating with the town. Jane Ellis, the RSC's Communications Manager, soon realised what had to be done. 'We were in a Transformation project group meeting and Vikki Heywood said something on the lines of,

"Winning planning permission for this project will depend on how well we consult."

'I remember walking out with Roger Mortlock and saying, "That's you and me then".'

There had been no extensive consultation on The Courtyard Theatre because the scheme had to be driven forward at speed, a fact that revived old suspicions about the autocratic RSC. That experience led to a determination that consultation on the RST makeover should be as thorough as possible. Ellis and Mortlock went out to talk to anyone who would listen – taxi drivers,

Open Day visitors examine a model of the new RST

The graffiti wall at the 2005 Open Day

An actor waits for his cue in the cramped backstage dock

Community Sunday tour: unsuspecting visitors are crammed into tight spaces backstage

bed and breakfast owners, residents of retirement homes, children in schools. As they considered how the views of local people could be relayed to the Company, an initial attempt at public consultation was launched at the RSC's Open Day in April 2005. Plans and models were set up in the circle bar of the still-functioning RST. Tom Piper, the Company's Associate Designer, was among those who spent hours listening to opinions. 'A lot of theatres are designed without consulting the people who are going to use them,' Piper said that day. 'We are hoping to create a new holy space here. We are creating more than a municipal hall.'

A graffiti wall had been set up in the RST on which anyone was free to scrawl comments about The Courtyard (on which work was about to begin) and the transformed RST (whose architects had just been appointed). Visitors were not slow to reach for the felt-tip pens. 'Please don't modernise too much – the building is beautiful just as it is,' wrote one. 'If it ain't broke, don't fix it,' added another. 'The play's the thing. The shell doesn't matter,' said a third.

Some were more concerned with practical matters such as 'comfy seats: some plays can be hard on the bottom'. (There's probably a PhD thesis in that: which of Shakespeare's plays is most likely to cause nether-end distress? *Hamlet*, because it's long? *Troilus and Cressida*, because it makes both brain and buttocks hurt?)

'More leg room, please,' cried a tall playgoer; 'A few more ladies' toilets for the interval,' added a woman who had clearly spent too long in a loo queue.

Someone asked for 'an Elizabethan theatre with 21st century facilities', which seemed a reasonable request.

Ellis and Mortlock also introduced Community Sundays on which a short talk would be followed by a tour of the RST and the Swan; the aim was to make clear to up to 200 people at a time why the building had to be changed for the better. 'We took them between the RST and the Swan and made them stand in the really small space [the soundproof docks] in which actors would wait before going on stage,' said Ellis. 'We explained that these were the conditions in which actors had to work. We rammed more and more people into the space and then shut the door. They began to sweat – and to understand.'

Ellis and Mortlock had begun to draw up a list of groups that ought to be consulted; it became very long. 'We ran an appeal in the *Stratford Herald* to bring in local residents,' said Ellis. 'We had a desire and ambition to make sure that lack of consultation was not going to be the reason the Transformation project did not get through the planning process. I didn't want anyone to tell me at the end that we had not spoken to enough people.'

Three weeks after the Open Day in April 2005, the RSC announced the creation of a community forum to be

1.2

chaired by Sir Brian Follett, former Vice-Chancellor of the University of Warwick, Stratford resident and President of the Stratford Society. The forum would meet four times a year to 'act as a constructive, independent voice for the RSC, representing the people who live and work in Stratford as well as those who visit the theatres'. The forum would also keep an eye on The Courtyard Theatre as it was being built.

Rab Bennetts and Simon Erridge from Bennetts Associates welcomed the forum (which included HOOT representatives). 'We had often been involved in consultation before but not on the scale introduced by the RSC,' said Erridge. 'It was new to us to have a community forum that was so well constructed and representative rather than a public meeting to which we were invited. There were some difficult questions but there was also an understanding of the process we as architects went through. We showed them how the scheme was evolving every couple of months. We always told them the truth and took them through every step of the way. We probably had eight or nine meetings and I think we won their confidence.'

Heywood, Boyd and Project Director Peter Wilson all turned up to answer questions and give information at various forum meetings. 'Sir Brian was adamant that the forum had to have a reporting structure right through to the Board because he saw it as a very important group,' said Ellis. 'There was quite a lot of nervousness internally about setting up the group – certainly about having people who might be seen as our opponents on it.'

The Rev Martin Gorick, vicar of Holy Trinity and a member of the forum, said the RSC did listen to members' contrasting views. 'The key opposition people were all included – the ones who had been the most vociferous opponents of the whole process were prominent members of the forum. I thought it was a very clever stroke.'

There was much discussion of the controversial tower. But the thrust stage was a no-go area: the RST was going to have one and that was that.

In the autumn after the forum got under way, the RSC also commissioned wider consultation in Stratford from Opinion Leader Research. The results, published early in 2006, suggested that local people wanted a landmark building that was open and welcoming and sympathetic to the town's character.

Mortlock and Ellis had also recognised the importance in the town of the independently-owned *Stratford-upon-Avon Herald* and resolved to give its editor Chris Towner unique access to the Transformation story as it unfolded. Towner and the *Herald* had, over the years, offered measured and not uncritical support to the RSC. Now editor and paper were faced with the tricky job of reporting accurately the Company's plans and local residents' reactions to them.

'There has been a suspicion about the RSC that it is not one of us, is not a Stratford organisation,' said Towner. 'I can see the difficulties there: it is an international organisation that happens to have its heart in a market town in Warwickshire. So a lot of things the RSC does are misunderstood or regarded with deep suspicion by local people and there is a fear that the Company may undermine the Shakespeare economy.

'The relationship goes in cycles. The RSC goes through a period of cosying up to the people of Stratford and then – and this is how it is perceived – when it has got the people of Stratford on board for a project, it quickly sidelines them while it pursues its national and international interests.'

The community forum: an independent voice

Snowbound Stratford: the view over Clopton Bridge as seen from the tower in December 2010

But no one, as far as he can remember, ever complained about the community forum. His own complaint was that he was not allowed access to it. 'From our point of view it was a bit strange. There would be 100 or more people who had detailed knowledge of the RSC's plans that we didn't have.'

The community forum met for the last time in December 2006 (but lived on as a community group, with Follett once more as Chairman). Before the meeting began, Jane Ellis and RSC colleagues carried in the latest model of the transformed RST, one that showed how Bennetts had raised the roof, creating an extra storey and with it the new restaurant with views over the river and beyond. One possible ill omen that night was when part of the tower fell off the architects' model. But an instant repair was made with a discreet splodge of Blu-Tack.

There were continued grumblings of discontent about the tower but most forum members were warmly supportive of the final design for the building. As the meeting and the forum came to an end, Follett reflected: 'Over the last year, a lot of us have looked at the Royal Shakespeare Theatre differently and seen it as pretty horrible. It is not the beautiful building we thought it was two years ago.'

13

Like several key members of the Transformation project team, Andy Hayles had bad memories of the balcony at the Royal Shakespeare Theatre: he had fallen asleep on those wickedly uncomfortable seats during a performance of *Measure for Measure* while studying for his A levels.

Twenty-two years later, Hayles was back in Stratford working on the interior design of The Courtyard with colleagues from his newly-formed theatre design company Charcoalblue. He was also hoping to win the contract to work on the auditorium of the new-look RST.

Rab Bennetts was curious about the name when, in 2005, he joined a 20-strong panel to interview Hayles for the RST job. 'I knew that Rab was an Arsenal supporter so when he asked,

Different models for the RST auditorium
prepared by Charcoalblue

"Why Charcoalblue?", I just said without thinking, "Because we hate Arsenal".'

Examining auditorium models at
the offices of Bennetts Associates

After a period of struggle, Hayles and his colleagues eventually decided to name themselves after the colour filters used on theatre lights and their working title became No Colour Blue until they discovered the name was the copyright of a leading gel supplier. 'We had to register our company name the next day,' remembered Hayles. 'That night I was at home listening to a Wayne Shorter jazz album and track two was called the Charcoal Blues. That was it. I registered the name before I even told my colleagues.'

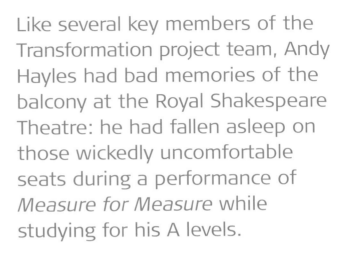

13

Charcoalblue was still a very young company but Hayles and his team thought they had an outside chance of winning the RST contract, not least because of their work on The Courtyard. The first interview went well and they were invited for a second. 'It was much more formal. Much scarier. We were down to the last two but it didn't go as well as the first interview. But I think we did enough to convince them we could pull it off.'

Rab Bennetts, despite Hayles' contemptuous comments about his football team, was totally convinced. 'They were terrific; their ideas, their understanding of the whole scheme at Stratford and theatre design in general was just spot-on. By the time we started working with them, The Courtyard was already mapped out. We carried on with the work we were doing on the RST and they with theirs and fused the two together.'

Hayles celebrated winning the contract by getting drunk. Once he had sobered up, he had, as with The Courtyard, to form that crucial working relationship between architect (well-established with a portfolio that included corporate headquarters and university buildings) and theatre designer (young upstart with a fast-growing reputation for originality). 'Some architects will show you a blob on a drawing and ask you to fit in 1,200 seats,' said Hayles. 'And once you have made the sightlines work, they come and tell you what colour the walls and seats are to be. Other architects will say they want to learn from our experience, to work with us.

'Both ways are fine but we prefer working the second way and on the RST it was much more collaborative than I had expected. Rab was very cool about it. He told me that we had the experience of The Courtyard and he was not going to tell us what would work and what wouldn't.

'The fashioning of the RST auditorium became a good-natured battle.'

In broad terms, Bennetts looked after the detailing of the auditorium – the metalwork, the finishes, the look and feel of the space; Charcoalblue was responsible for sightlines and technical matters including machinery, winches, lifts and lighting. Decisions about the shape of the auditorium, however, appear to have been taken through discussion and sometimes argument.

The two balconies in The Courtyard curve sensuously around the thrust stage. When thinking began in earnest about the interior look of the new RST, the RSC's own artistic team, led by Michael Boyd and Tom Piper, considered both a curved gallery front and a faceted version, as suggested by Bennetts. Models were made and the faceted look, like the rude mechanicals' production of *Pyramus and Thisbe*, was preferred.

Sir Peter Hall reviews auditorium models with Michael Boyd and team at the Rose Theatre, Kingston. From left to right: Michael Boyd, Sir Peter Hall, Alasdair McKenzie (Bennetts Associates), Gavin Green (Charcoalblue) and Tom Piper

That preference was passed to Charcoalblue. Bennetts liked the more geometrical, faceted look, not least because it suited the tighter dimensions of the RST, where the auditorium would be a metre narrower than at The Courtyard. Charcoalblue, happy with facets, produced a layout based on an 11-sided figure, introducing a short side between each long side to create a 22-sided geometry.

By happy chance, the 11-sided form was almost identical in every respect, including its dimensions, to the shape of the Rose Theatre on London's Bankside, the remains of which were uncovered by archaeologists in 1989. (The theatre was reborn in the film *Shakespeare In Love*.) Bennetts and Erridge debated for some time whether that shape had been the deliberate choice of an Elizabethan theatre consultant or whether the setting-out had gone slightly wonky. They also savoured the romantic notion of creating an auditorium almost identical to the one in which impresario Philip Henslowe had staged Christopher Marlowe's *Doctor Faustus*, *The Jew of Malta* and *Tamburlaine the Great*, Thomas Kyd's *The Spanish Tragedy* and Shakespeare's *Henry VI, Part I* and *Titus Andronicus*.

In the end, logic triumphed over romance and Bennetts settled on a 12-sided shape. 'We wondered what would happen if we made the geometry more regular so that the sides could then be parallel to the outside shell of the building,' said Bennetts. 'We tried it out and the adjustments were so marginal that we thought it was worth going for the more regular shape.'

One key element in the design of the RST was the creation of a sense of compression, which contrasted with the lofty airiness of The Courtyard. Michael Boyd was emphatic that he did not want 'too much air in the room', an auditorium with seats too big and aisles too wide. 'There was a feeling coming from Michael that

The new RST auditorium

the auditorium should be intensified, the kind of auditorium that Shakespeare might recognise,' said Bennetts. 'We were very engaged by that. There was a design session with Charcoalblue round the table at our office and someone commented, "What if the roof were brought right down?" That turned out to be so much more appropriate in terms of scale.'

Now the control room is up in the roof and staff look down through a hole in the ceiling that looms low, lower than in The Courtyard, over the second tier. Lower down, the impact on sightlines was huge: the call for compression caused great problems that took time to solve.

Bennetts and Erridge found themselves caught up in another debate that had not happened when they designed Hampstead Theatre: how would the seats be laid out in the auditorium? 'There was a lot of talk with Michael and the project team about the community you create between aisles,' said Bennetts. 'That also influenced the geometry a bit.'

13

Then there was the crucial question of how the galleries should be held up: self-supporting (as in the old RST) or with columns (as in The Courtyard)? 'To have had cantilevered, free-spanning balconies would have been a little bit too shiny modern and lacking in character,' said Bennetts. 'We felt very strongly that in architectural terms columns bring the space in and give that sense of compression Michael wanted. You couldn't have them right on the front row because they would get in the way. But the next row back was possible.

'We were told that we could not put columns in a new theatre because they were bound to create sightline problems. But we came to the conclusion that we could minimise the problem by making sure the columns were as small as possible and in the right places. The benefits of columns outweighed disadvantages.'

The Courtyard's columns were circular; those in the RST are cruciform in section and their apparent volume changes depending on the angle from which they are seen. They remain raw and unpainted, their steeliness unconcealed. Equally plain oak boards fixed to the concrete back wall that embraces the auditorium should solve the acoustic blips experienced in The Courtyard.

'To reach the auditorium, you pass into the gap between the rather fine 1930s foyer and the drum wall surrounding the auditorium. It's a rugged, tall, ambiguous, inside-outside space and that is the opposite of what happens in many theatres,' said Bennetts. 'With its unfinished steel and sawn timber planks, the auditorium is slightly rougher and more rugged than the original Art Deco foyers. It always seemed to us that, in most theatres, the experience becomes more luxurious as one moves from the foyer into the auditorium. But at the RST that experienced is reversed.'

The circle in the new RST

A ghost in the wall
of the new auditorium

This theatre would never pretend that it was brand new; it was a reconstruction, a redevelopment, a moving on to a new stage, literal and metaphorical, in the RSC's history.

There was much debate about the three-storey back wall of the foyer. The simplest plan would have been to repair, plaster and paint it. But Tom Piper was convinced the wall should not be tidied up with a few gallons of magnolia emulsion from B&Q. 'As more and more of the building became clean and finished with new surfaces, that threw into a nice tension the old surfaces which we wanted to leave relatively raw. I didn't want anyone to say, "These old bits of wall are a little bit messy so let's tidy them up". I had a theatrical rather than an architectural approach in mind.'

Piper's aim was to preserve the wall's history, including the imprints of an old staircase and rooms left behind when the auditorium was demolished. 'I wanted to use a bit of scenic art magic to make the whole wall feel

And when Love speaks,

coherent and beautiful, especially for those who love distressed paint texture.'

His other *coup de décor* was to fix a group of seats from the old balcony on the preserved wall in the new restaurant, as a reminder of how far from the stage some members of the audience had once sat.

Andy Hayles said three things would hit people when they entered the new auditorium. 'It's smaller. Second, the galleries are faceted and the RST is more robust, with a sense that it will be here forever. The Courtyard – miraculously – has never felt like that; it creaks a bit and the steel box makes noises when warmed by the sun.

'Third, I like to think that it feels like a more cohesive whole and that for the first time, the RSC is going to have a large theatre with the feel of a single room.'

The upper circle joins the proscenium arch

The relic wall at the back of the Art Deco foyer

Computer-generated cut-away
image of the transformed theatres

1.4

In September 2006 the RSC's project committee, chaired by Susie Sainsbury, prepared to meet to approve Bennetts Associates' design for the entire scheme, including a new suite of offices for RSC staff behind the old Union Club on Chapel Lane.

At an earlier gathering in Sainsbury's home, the plans and a model had already been shown to the Company's international committee, representing major donors who had given the RSC more than £100,000. All that remained now was to rubber-stamp the scheme at the meeting, held in the Westminster office of Sainsbury's husband Lord Sainsbury, and send it to Stratford-on-Avon District Council before the Christmas break.

The architects Rab Bennetts and Simon Erridge were present for the first part of the meeting to give their final presentation. 'There was a slightly muted reaction and I could feel that things were not quite right,' said Bennetts. 'I said to Simon on the way down the street afterwards, "That wasn't exactly a ringing endorsement was it?"

The original plan for the RST, before the roof was raised

And he said, "I wonder what's up".'

What was up soon became apparent as the meeting continued without Bennetts and Erridge. Sainsbury was not happy. 'I just knew we had got it wrong. It just looked as though we had tinkered with the building. There was nothing bold or new about it. Bennetts had done what we had asked them to do, which was to put the auditorium in the middle and make use of the Art Deco spaces. But it didn't have any excitement about it. There was nothing that said this was different in any way. I should have rung Christopher [Bland] on the morning of that meeting and said what my position was. But because we needed to accept the design at that point, I knew Christopher would have bullied me out of it. The only thing to do was not to tell anyone.'

Bland, as Sainsbury remembers it, said that this was a wonderful day because the committee had before it a scheme all could accept. Taking a deep breath, Sainsbury then said: 'I don't think we can. I'm perfectly prepared to resign but I can't put my name to this. I think we've got it wrong. Or at least we haven't got it right.'

Bland went purple; Peter Wilson and Vikki Heywood both went white. None had had any forewarning of this crisis. 'I was not the most popular person in SW1 that particular day,' said Sainsbury. 'Christopher said it was too late to change the scheme. We would miss our planning slot and any changes would cost us money.'

Then came another unexpected intervention, this time from Michael Boyd. He had not colluded with Sainsbury but said he agreed with her and could not back the scheme as it stood.

The scheme was not approved. After the meeting, Bland summoned Sainsbury and Boyd to Lord Sainsbury's private office. Heywood was also there. 'Christopher was installed in David's [Sainsbury's] chair while Michael and I stood. He was incandescent with rage,' said Sainsbury. 'I'd never seen anybody quite so cross. He accused us of complicity and asked us what we had got to say for ourselves.'

'I was furious with them because it was outrageous behaviour and they left me dangling out on a limb, as they will admit,' said Bland. 'I right-royally bollocked them afterwards and they quite appropriately apologised.

I had no objection to their disagreeing but for them to disagree after I had said to the committee, "This is it. Let's go ahead" was just bad and irritating. It was a poor way to behave.'

'What followed were probably the worst three months of my life,' said Sainsbury. 'We were going to miss our planning application slot and would have to apply for permission just after Christmas. If we didn't get the scheme to the planning committee by the middle of January, the whole sequence was completely stuffed.'

Boyd called Bennetts and Erridge and suggested that they had shown too much respect to Elisabeth Scott's building; had been insufficiently bold. Sainsbury also rang. 'She was absolutely terrified that we might quit,' said Rab Bennetts. 'That had never crossed my mind. If we had banged the table and thrown our toys out of the pram and resigned, that would have been a bit uncharacteristic.

'And within 24 hours we decided they were right and that we should have another go.'

→

Sketch showing the revised plan for the roof

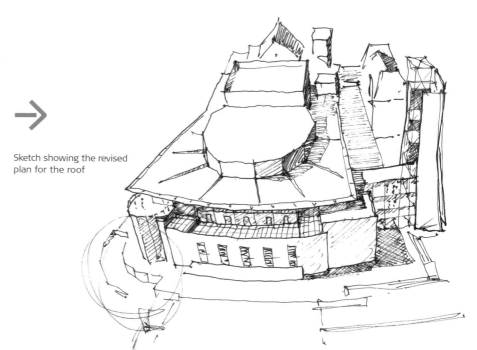

The site at night during the construction of the new roof

There was no question of ripping up the entire plan and starting again. Most of the scheme – the auditorium, the public spaces, the tower – was fine but the front of the building looking on to the Bancroft Gardens was seen as being too self-effacing, too similar to what it had always been. Bennetts and Erridge had sensed that themselves but had felt too constrained by the very tight budget to do something more radical. 'If we had let loose a bit earlier, we would have been seriously criticised,' said Bennetts. 'Was it a failure of imagination on our part or a pragmatic response to the tight budget? I think it was much more the latter. It was a very easy change and I sketched out something quite quickly. It seemed to be a very substantial change in perception without much damage, except to the budget.'

The Board sanctioned the additional cost and the fund-raising target was adjusted upwards. 'If our scheme was too self-effacing, we had to do something bolder,' said Bennetts. 'There was no other way to go. I'm glad we did it. We could have kicked ourselves and should have told them ourselves at the meeting that we were not happy with it.'

Bennetts' new sketches doubled the height of the top floor and floated a huge canopy roof over the whole theatre to give it a new skyline.

The familiar façade of the RST would be significantly changed as the 21st century asserted itself more in

1.4

a design that showed less deference to the 1930s. 'We had been too pragmatic and had listened a bit too much to the voices of the conservation lobby. The RST was OK as a building but it was not a great piece of architecture,' said Bennetts. 'So why be quite so respectful?'

The theatre restaurant would be in an airy space under a roof now raised three metres, with floor-to-ceiling windows giving views of the river and the town. 'The restaurant breaks all the rules,' said Bennetts. 'It's not on the ground floor, it's up at the top and you can't see the far end of it when you come in – you have to go and find it. All kinds of things are difficult about it but it's an amazing space. And it links spatially to the foyers below through the gap round the drum that surrounds the auditorium.'

Stratford's planning committee unanimously approved the revised scheme in March 2007 and the Transformation project was back on track. Bland accepts that Sainsbury and Boyd were right, even if the way they voiced their concerns was wrong. 'We wound up in a good place and I think the creative tension of the agreement and disagreement was pretty good. I think Bennetts would accept that collectively we have been a demanding and difficult client, but also a good client.'

Rab Bennetts' view is that he and his team at times

needed 'the thick skin of a rhino and the patience of a saint'

in their dealings with the Gang of Five. 'At some meetings, it was really difficult to stay calm. If they had chosen a different architect, there would have been a falling out or a massive row. But we were quite patient. We were working with a group of people who had different tastes. Michael likes grunge and Susie likes minimalist modern. How do you reconcile those? It was really difficult but it worked.

'Christopher was an active Chairman. Meetings finished on time and no one left the room until decisions were taken. He thumped the table and shouted but decisions were made. He was not an easy man to get on with but he made things happen. And that's what he was there for.'

Sketch of the restaurant interior

The new restaurant with restored arches

The bridge linking the auditorium and the upper circle bar

Scene of destruction:
the walls come down
on a poster-lined corridor
in the RST

1.5

A few days after the last performance of a Shakespeare play in the old RST auditorium in March 2007, the Royal Shakespeare Company's own staff moved in to do a soft strip, the process of tidying up and clearing away that had to be completed before demolition teams could move in to bash the building about.

The soft-strippers picked up old playbills, props and other bits of detritus, significant and trivial, accumulated during 75 years in the life of a great theatre.

They searched dusty shelves and forgotten cupboards and made some fascinating finds.

But one relic they had not expected to come across was hidden down a ledge of brickwork at the back of the proscenium arch: a Webley revolver, the type of pistol favoured by Britain's soldiers for more than 70 years.

This was not a prop but the real thing, possibly concealed in readiness for an appropriate murderous moment by a long-gone aggrieved spear carrier intent on the assassination of some particularly demanding director.

'It looked like hell rather than a building site': the auditorium is demolished from the top down

15

The police were called at once. Had there been a significant delay, either Vikki Heywood or Michael Boyd, or both, could have been banged up for possession of a firearm, an unfortunate turn of events that could have brought the Company some unwelcome publicity.

After the soft strip came the heritage strip.

Specialist contractors removed all the fine wood that had been used in the construction of the RST. They also removed most of the door frames and doors, plus hinges, handles and knobs, and stored them off-site in what became a door library. Many of those doors (some reversed in order to make their elegance more apparent) have returned to the theatre, but not necessarily in their original locations because some of those locations no longer exist.

What could not be removed, especially in the listed Art Deco parts of the building, was protected. The fountain court was boarded up and sent to sleep for three years and time itself was frozen: the foyer's large clock stopped at 12 minutes past 12. The foyer and the circle bar above were cleared of clutter – poster panels, ice cream freezers, programme points and shop stands – and acquired again the stylish simplicity of their early days.

The gents' toilet between stalls and circle levels was at this stage still intact, although all doors had been removed from its cubicles. In the auditorium, all seats had been removed but the tiers on which they had been anchored remained.

The strip took longer than expected. There was a last minute decision to hang on to a huge central vacuum cleaner installed in a big room under a set of stairs. Cleaning staff could connect to it from any part of the building and it was valued for its labour-saving efficiency. It is now safely stored off-site in Stratford.

The roof is removed: 'it looked as though a bomb had gone off'

The first cut: a muncher bites into the Waterside façade

'There was some stuff we could not take out until demolition had begun because we could not get to it,' added Simon Harper, Deputy Project Director. 'There is still stuff in there that, with hindsight, we should have taken out. But we didn't see it at the time.'

As 2007 progressed, the number of workers and trades on site began to increase steadily. Instead of appointing a single contractor, the RSC had individual contracts with many trades and had appointed Mace, a company specialising in commercial management services.

Stripping gave way to heavy demolition at the start of October. Many found it a shock to see the physical reality of what had until then only been planned on paper. The first sign of the scale of what was to come was a three-storey vertical gash in the wall facing Waterside. It looked as if the theatre had been struck by an appallingly precise earthquake. Windows, several without glass, hung open; a forgotten chair loitered in an empty room. Soon a monster 125-tonne super-muncher arrived and began chomping its way through the wall to the left of the crack. It's said that observers (whether they were local residents, tourists, theatregoers or RSC members is not on record) wept as the destruction advanced, exposing a wall of RSC posters on the senior management corridor.

'People should have realised what was going to happen,' said Wilson. 'We had gone through all the explanations about why we were taking down that side wall, which wasn't much loved.

'People made an intellectual commitment to the idea of change but didn't make the emotional connection until they saw the wall falling.'

The familiar front of the theatre was detached from the ruins of the old auditorium and stood alone, forlornly supported by a frame of blue steel girders. Round the corner on the river side, a mini-muncher casually bit chunks out of the terrace café and cast aside the rubble. The destruction continued above the café in what had once been Quarto's restaurant, with fallen masonry pushed through a specially-made hole in the floor. Elsewhere, drills roared as the systematic wrecking went deafeningly on.

Soon the side balconies in the auditorium were reduced to their bare timber supports and the stage was no more than a steel skeleton on which only a well-balanced Hamlet could survive. It was an eerie space, well suited to a director considering a grunge *Macbeth*, whose ambitious hero could have run up and down the retained backstage cast iron spiral staircase to slaughter Duncan.

More than 150 square metres of the actor-scarred teak floor from the old stage were later recycled for the floor of the new foyers. Members of the audience now find themselves literally treading the old boards and could enjoy an interval ice cream on the very spot, if they could find it, where Kenneth Branagh's Hamlet said 'The rest is silence' and expired.

The serious destruction began when large mobile cranes arrived in early November 2007 to remove the steel roof

The five-tonne roof girders are removed

The fly tower loses its roof; the auditorium space is now almost free of rubble

trusses, each of which weighed five tonnes and was two metres deep. (Bits of the trusses were salvaged and later used to support benches in the new square by the tower.) Then work began 'to bring the roof to the foundation', as Cominius says in *Coriolanus*. The auditorium was destroyed from the top down, with the ceiling and various air conditioning ducts allowed to drop to the stalls below. 'Up to then, we had done the work surgically and neatly,' said Wilson. 'Now it looked as if a bomb had gone off.'

'It looked like hell rather than a building site,' added Harper. 'It didn't look ordered and structured in any way. It was as if the building had collapsed, as if something had gone wrong.'

This preliminary work eventually allowed what was left of the original stage machinery, with its lifts and trucks, to be removed. Before it went, Wilson and Harper invited former production managers, technical directors and stage staff back to the theatre to have one last nostalgic go at hand-cranking it.

The auditorium walls came down early in 2008 and the roof of the fly tower was removed a little later, in preparation for the installation of new fans that would suck out smoke in case of fire.

On the river side of the building, it was found that nothing of any significance, apart from minimal foundations and the walls of the Swan, appeared to be holding up the old dressing room block – which suggests that at any time since 1932 the cream of the acting profession could have been dumped into the Avon. The only realistic option was to demolish the whole thing, insert new piles and build a new suite of dressing rooms.

Instead of using concrete floors, consulting engineers Buro Happold suggested the use of cross-laminated timber panels, commonly used in parts of Europe but then still a novelty in Britain. The 250mm thick planks, like giant pieces of plywood, are three times lighter than concrete, which had several benefits: lighter foundations, a lighter steel frame and an extra floor for the building. And it all cost less, too.

The construction of a basement in the new auditorium presented possibly the biggest challenge of the whole project. 'We thrive on challenges and tricky situations,' said Andrew Wylie of Buro Happold. 'There was no benefit to be seen in flapping. We didn't want the engineering to limit the artistic potential of this space.'

The old RST had a basement under the original stage, with a shallower orchestra pit between it and the auditorium. These two were to be combined and then extended under the new thrust stage to create a large hole seven metres deep (roughly the height of a two-storey house) and big enough to conceal, before a dramatic entrance from below, a tall actor sitting on a throne while carrying a long spear. But joining up the three segments and making the whole thing watertight was a complex task, especially as the water table was only 1.82 metres below ground level.

'Next to a river, you don't just dig a big hole,'

added Wylie. 'You have to do lots of temporary works and lots of excavations first. We needed to understand the construction of the basement under the 1932 fly tower; what effect it had on the ground around it, and make sure that building a new basement would not cause the fly tower to topple. We also had to be certain that the existing basement, which had never leaked, did not start cracking or flexing or letting in water.'

While plays were still in performance at the old RST, engineers seized a window of opportunity to remove

Two aspects of the back wall of the Art Deco foyer

some seats from the stalls, drive a rig through the front door and sink a borehole beneath where the thrust stage would eventually be.

Later excavations during the reconstruction of the auditorium revealed that the space in front of the original basement had been filled with junk, including fractured concrete, old steel and building materials. Early in 2008, piles were sunk through unstable river gravel, silts and alluvial deposits and into rocks known as the Mercia Mudstone. 'We had to be sure the water would not get in through the walls nor go underneath the basement and up into it,' said Wylie.

But piles could not be driven right up to the wall of the existing basement. A plug of grout had to be injected to fill the gap. It was made of free-flowing concrete mixed with the clay mineral bentonite to make it impermeable. Six temporary wells pumped water non-stop to lower the water table while a concrete lining wall was built inside the piles. No water was pumped into the river but ran instead into a settlement tank and then into a nearby sewer. 'It was crystal clear,' said Jim Gillespie, Senior Construction Manager for Mace. 'We could have bottled it and made some money for the RSC.'

At the bottom of the basement there is now a concrete base 1.8 metres thick and strong enough, according to Buro Happold, to resist upward water pressure equivalent to the weight of two fully-laden 747 jumbo jets. The river should never now intrude on *King Lear*, although it could come in handy for Cleopatra's barge.

This tricky basement work took until February 2009. Elsewhere, progress was much faster. By June 2008, two huge white tower cranes, one in what had been the car park at the front of the theatre, the other in the yard of the Swan, were ready to swing materials to any part of the building. July that year was the busiest

month so far: 5,276 people worked on the site, totting up 42,826 person hours; almost three quarters of a million working hours had been clocked up since counting began in October 2007.

At the end of August 2008, a start was made on the tower. But before the builders could go upwards, they had to go downwards: 22 concrete piles were sunk 16 metres into the ground and then connected together by a concrete cap that incorporated the pit into which the tower's lift would sink.

Specialist bricklayers from contractors Lesterose arrived at about the same time and, using mortar identical to that used during the original construction, began restoring the brickwork on the theatre's riverside wall, which had been cruelly damaged when the café was built. The semi-circular concrete wall that embraced the new auditorium was complete by the autumn of 2008, and at the end of September a 38-tonne mobile crane dropped the creamy yellow steel roof trusses, each 30 metres long and weighing more than 30 tonnes, into place; they were welded together while still hanging from the jib. When released and slotted precisely into place an admiring crowd of public and builders in the Bancroft Gardens applauded and cheered.

By November 2008 the auditorium was beginning to look like a theatre. From the centre of the upper circle, where the cheapest seats would be, a visitor could look down on a compact one-room playhouse and imagine the strutting and fretting to come. A month later, the new theatre reached its highest point and, with a final spade or two of concrete on the roof, was topped out with the traditional ceremony. The scheme was halfway to completion – and on time.

Sparks fly as work on the RST progresses

INTERVAL 03

Richard III sat in an empty bath ('My kingdom for some water!') when the RSC threw open the new-look Royal Shakespeare Theatre (or parts of it) on a sunny February Sunday towards the end of the long, hard winter of 2009-10.

Jonathan Slinger, who played the murderous monarch in the 2006-08 *Histories* cycle at The Courtyard and in London, settled into the tub as he examined the new suite of dressing rooms (each with its own balcony and view of the Avon) at the transformed theatre.

He was one of more than 100 actors, both distinguished alumni and members of the current ensemble, who came to catch a glimpse of how construction work was progressing.

The actors were pampered with jacket potatoes and coffee set out on tables on the familiar old boards beneath the fly tower before being urged to venture forward on to the new thrust stage. Had Luciana from *The Comedy of Errors* been there, she might then have instructed them to 'gaze where you should, and that will clear your sight'.

Gaze they did and, like those who followed, marvelled. Slowly they found their bearings, seeking first the outline of the old auditorium and then beginning to absorb the multi-faceted shape of the new one, much of which was shrouded in ghostly white plastic to protect its wood-lined walls from the damp.

Tim Pigott-Smith, a Company member from 1972-75 and now a member of the RSC Board, was among the gazers. 'I used to come here to the theatre in the late 1950s as a kid,' he told a television crew. 'I was in the two-bob seats at the top of the balcony and I thought you had to be small to be an actor because the stage was so far away. [Now] it's a completely different relationship.'

Michael Boyd was on hand in his high-visibility vest to enthuse, and to muse that there were enough actors, directors and designers in the building at that moment to 'put on a show right here and right now'.

The new RST, he said, might have a one-room auditorium but its construction did not signify a puritanical retreat from design theatre. 'You can if you wish bring the entire Forest of Arden down from up there [in the ceiling]. You can also push up the entire Forest of Arden from below in the seven-metre basement.'

The actors turned to look at the fly tower when Boyd pointed out that it was still where it had always been, propping up the building. He spoke then about the storage capacity in the new theatre, a fact that would help keep alive a large repertory of productions. 'I feel very strongly that, long after I'm gone, this will continue to be a defining feature of what is special about the RSC, that this is a Company that shows a range of work that a group of artists can produce and develop over time.'

Boyd, now well into his passionate stride, then described how the transformed theatre would set out to greet the town rather than, as previously, face the Bancroft Gardens like a fortress. As for the tower: 'I like the vulgarity of us shamelessly and brazenly going out to be a tourist attraction. The tower is big and tall, beautifully made. It is going to be a major piece of fly paper for people who normally just feed the ducks, go for a row on the river and eat ice creams. Hopefully more of them will be tempted to come up the tower and look at four counties and into the Vale of Evesham.'

The new tower mirrors the old one that had stood by the first Shakespeare Memorial Theatre and contained water that was to be released in case of fire; but when fire came in 1926, the tower burned down before it could extinguish its own flames. Elisabeth's Scott's riverside façade has been decluttered and restored; the Avon itself, with its new riverside path, has been 'reintroduced as part of our lifeblood'; and the RST and the Swan have been connected by a new colonnade, with views through the Swan's now unblocked carriage arch down to Holy Trinity.

Not much had changed at the Swan: new seats, more flying space and a farewell to the 'ludicrous sound-proof docks, upstage left and right' in which actors waited to go on stage. But as the actors set off on their tour, still looking around like Miranda in her brave new world, they found that the Swan, for a place where nothing much was happening, was a bit of a mess: no familiar benches but lots of steel ducting, scaffolding and boxes. But familiar Swan backstage graffiti remained: 'Dicko is stupid'; 'Shufflebottom 2001'.

The visitors were guided upstairs to the dressing rooms (where Slinger took his dry plunge), which were much approved, especially the spacious children's room with its two views of the river. Some were clearly eyeing it up as a potential studio flat before they circled back, between the new beautifully-bricked drum wall and the back of the original foyer, to the colonnade.

As they left and non-actors queued to get in, Julian Glover, who first worked in Stratford with Laurence Olivier and Michael Redgrave before the RSC was born, stood like a man bowled over. 'Michael Boyd is absolutely right when he says the old lingers in the building, despite the fact that you can hardly see what it was. But you can still see the proscenium arch and all those ghosts are really still in it. That sounds a silly actory thing to say but I don't think it is; the whole essence of the space is still here despite this wonderful modernisation.

'I did eight seasons here. A lot of us, when we heard they were going to do this, asked: "Why change it?" It had always worked and it worked for Olivier and Edith Evans. But I am now persuaded. Now, my God, I'd love to get on to that new stage.'

Down at the Dirty Duck, Richard Plantagenet and the Duke of Bedford, also veterans of the *Histories* company that had travelled from *Richard II* to *Richard III*, were having a drink in the almost-spring sun. Like Glover, Clive Wood (Plantagenet) wanted to be in the limelight at the new RST.

'I live in Stratford so I have watched the theatre grow and it's very exciting to think that one day I might be on that stage. I had affection for the old theatre; I grew up in rep, performing in proscenium arches all the time and there's a place for that still. But this is the way forward. Once you have experienced playing that kind of space, it's hard to go back. The *Histories* in The Courtyard were stunning.

'It's great to see those dressing rooms at last. We have had so many talks about them. Having light and air, and balconies, makes a huge difference to an actor; the chance to get some sun on your face – and somewhere to have a cigarette.'

Tom Hodgkins (Bedford), who played a gazetteer of other nobles including Westmoreland, Buckingham and Hastings, had had the distinction of speaking the first line ('Hung be the heavens with black: yield, day, to night!') of *Henry VI, Part I*, the first full production staged at The Courtyard.

He was not sure about the RST's tower, which for him bore a whiff of Canary Wharf. 'But it's great that what they have done to the theatre has been without compromise. Michael Boyd had a dream and they have gone for it.'

A final significant fact from Boyd's address to the actors and the public: 'There were 19 ladies' loos here before. Now there are 47.' Everyone cheered.

The concrete core of Bennetts Associates' new tower by the side of the Royal Shakespeare Theatre was finished by Christmas 2008 and was immediately dubbed 'the crematorium chimney' by some of Stratford's more cynical citizens.

Undaunted, the project team celebrated both the festive season and a significant achievement by fixing a giant illuminated star to the top, possibly in the hope that the completed tower would lead people to the theatre as the biblical star had led the three wise men to Bethlehem.

But not all was comfort and joy.

The excavation of the understage basement had caused many headaches and had threatened a significant hold-up. In the autumn of 2008, the project had suffered a major setback, not on site but at the premises of Trekwerk, the Dutch company contracted to assemble the winches that, once installed in the new RST's roof, would lower and raise both scenery and actors with the help of sophisticated computer control systems. ('Trekwerk,' boasts the company, 'moves everything on, behind, under and above your stage with passion.')

At 11pm on 2 October, a fire broke out at the company's factory in Weesp, south-east of Amsterdam, and raged for three hours, destroying most of the building and threatening to throw a major spanner into the RST works. Trekwerk was not fully back in business until the end of February 2009. 'We took a long time to recover from that fire,' said Peter Wilson, the Project Director. But the Transformation show had to go on.

Christmas 2008: the star on the tower's core shines over Stratford

The new basement: room for a tall king with a crown

THEATRES

1.6

The RSC star shone on into 2009, a year that began with a severe chill as temperatures dropped way below freezing. This created yet another headache: a damp-proof membrane had to be fixed to the tower's concrete core before the bricklayers could move in. But it could only be set in place in temperatures above 5°C.

Eventually the highly-skilled team was ready to start work on walls that would be load-bearing rather than a mere skin. They were ready to use engineering bricks, handmade in the Forest of Dean, which would be strong enough to take the immense weight of the tower. But work on test panels had shown that the mortar used to glue the bricks together dried slowly; wet and sloppy, it had often squeezed out between courses like soggy porridge. The problem was made even worse by the cold.

Progress was slow and made slower by the need to create walls with a three degree slope. To guide the bricklayers, a 'spider' was fixed to the top of the concrete core with piano wire suspended to ground level.

This innovation worked but the spider and wires had to be regularly removed to allow sections of the internal steel staircase to be dropped into place.

'That rigging and de-rigging caused the bricklaying to fall behind schedule,' said Wilson. 'But as the tower climbed higher, it became easier to build because there were far fewer bricks to lay at the narrower top of the tower.'

The bricklayers caught up but still took nine months to reach the summit. Elsewhere, work progressed well. By late spring 2009, the original foyer was joined to new walls and the steel girders that had propped it up were removed. By July, the big steelwork for the new roof, the colonnade and the new dressing room block was

September 2009:
the 20-tonne viewing
platform is lowered
into place

Drilling at stalls level

A crowd gathers to watch the platform being dropped into place (above);

the completed tower (below)

complete. More steel was brought in to create the circles and the technical gallery, and zinc cladding moved steadily round various parts of the theatre's exterior.

The building was now watertight, although there were to be annoying leaks on the fly tower, the restaurant roof and the top of the fountain staircase. None of these problems became a disaster. 'There was never a point when I asked myself, "How are we going to get out of this?",' said Simon Harper, Deputy Project Director. 'There was always someone who had a bright idea. The solution appeared almost at the same time as the nightmare arrived.'

The tower's viewing platform, weighing 20 tonnes and as big as one of the cottages on Waterside, was constructed at ground level and on 29 September 2009 a crowd in the Bancroft Gardens held its breath as a 300-tonne crane prepared to hoist it into position.

'We were all worried about whether the weather would scupper the lift,' said Simon Erridge, Bennetts Associates' Project Architect. 'If the wind had been too strong, there would have been a problem. But it was a bright, warm sunny day with virtually no breeze.

'The bottom bit of the lift was always going to be the trickiest because the platform was quite close to the theatre and site huts and at the furthest reach from the crane. As it rose, a bit of wind caught it and it started to rotate, which was fine but a bit heart-stopping when you were standing in the Bancroft seeing this huge thing turning round.'

The platform was lifted and dropped into place on top of the tower within an hour. The following (rather more windy) day, two 11.5-tonne prefabricated panels made of bricks fixed to concrete slabs were hoisted up and bolted to the sides of the platform. The first one fouled the zinc on top of the roof; the second was less troublesome.

Glass was installed later and by Christmas 2009 the 36-metre tower was complete and, as the scaffolding came down, Stratford's residents and visitors could see its gradual shift from octagon to square, a move that created triangles of fine brickwork, with sides that merged into a delicate stiletto point beneath the observation platform.

Floors for the stage, stalls and circle were laid and work began on the new square on Waterside and walkway by the Avon. Once the theatre was watertight, contractors moved in to start building internal walls, create 16 new dressing rooms (each with a view of the river), lay miles of cable and wiring, install the steelwork under the stage and start painting, a process that took many months.

Right at the beginning of the project, the Transformation team had decided that the heart of both the RST and the Swan should be the distinctive RSC red and that the colour should extend into back of house areas and dressing rooms.

But focus groups with people who did not come to the theatre had, perhaps surprisingly, found red off-putting and unwelcoming. So public spaces, bars and foyers were painted in blues and greys, colours that pay quiet homage to the RST's origins in the 1930s. 'You will probably find those colours in the paintings of Ben Nicholson or Paul Nash,' said Wilson. 'Three million people visit Stratford each year and we wanted to make the RST attractive to the two million who do not come to the theatre. We didn't want them to feel challenged or unwelcome.'

One exception to the blue/grey rule had been the ceiling of the rooftop restaurant, which was to be red. But it clashed horribly with the orange-brown brickwork of the drum wall and was repainted silver, with a shiny finish that should not disturb diners' enjoyment of their pre-play meals.

16

As 2009 slid into 2010, Britain found itself in the grip of its coldest winter for 30 years. Water froze in pipes on the RST site; there was no canteen and no hot food or drinks. The toilets also froze. Most staff braved the cold and kept working, nipping over the road to the public conveniences on Waterside when nature called.

It was still pretty chilly on 20 February when present and past RSC actors and 1,000 members of the public were allowed on to the new thrust stage (26 cm shorter and 20 cm narrower than that at The Courtyard) to glimpse the new auditorium, then largely shrouded in plastic. One sheet had been pulled back to reveal some of the unplaned oak panels (Hamlet would have called them rough-hewn) fixed to the auditorium wall. The actors saw more: they were guided upstairs to see (and approve) dressing rooms, now kitted out with basins and shelves with enough room for a high hat and doors wide enough for a full skirt.

They also caught a tantalising glimpse of the Swan, about whose renovations very little fuss had been made. The entire theatre was then in the process of being rewired and the air conditioning was changing from a top-down breeze to a bottom-up gentle cooling flow. This meant the ducts in the roof that had blown sometimes icy draughts down the necks of patrons in the second gallery could be removed to create new flying space.

The seats take their place in the RST

February 2010: members of the public and past and present RSC actors catch their first glimpse of the new auditorium

The good news for audiences was that something was being done about the puritanical bench seats that could prove trying by the fifth act of any Shakespeare play, let alone a full day of the three parts of *Henry VI*. The RSC's in-house team realised that the padding on the benches was very flat and intolerant of the human shape. In other theatres, they found similar seats were more comfortable because the seating pad was divided into two separate cushions. Similar pads, covered in an elegant brown cord, were then installed to give greater comfort to the average Swan bottom.

The RST's seats, designed by the Italian company Poltrona Frau, which produces elegant sofas and beds, were fitted in the early summer of 2010. The company also designs seats for Ferrari, Maserati and Alfa Romeo sports cars; its experience of designing seats for the chicanes of *Troilus and Cressida* is possibly more limited but it knows how to create comfort in tight spaces. The BBC's arts correspondent said the seats transported him more to a bus stop than a race track, but conceded that their primary function was to engage the audience in the action; Michael Boyd promised at a later press conference that they would offer greater comfort to the buttocks of audiences.

The backs of seats close to the stage lean back more to enable members of the audience to look up. Seats further back and higher up have less of a tilt because members of the audience will generally be looking down. Some seats at the back of upper levels are raised up and fitted with footrests to prevent the pins and needles induced by leg dangle.

But there was another reason for the different designs.

'Michael Boyd calls the theatre a democratic house because there are no bad seats,'

Ghosts in the floor: the old stage floorboards are laid in the foyer

New windows, made to the original design, in the Avon façade

The curtain winding around the outside wall of the RST auditorium

said Wilson. 'Because we have reduced the distance of seats from the stage and sightlines are more than adequate everywhere, the only way we can differentiate the price of seats is by how much space we leave for audience bottoms.'

The cheapest of 24 types of seat are 450 mm wide with no arm rest; pay a little more and you acquire an arm rest and your own defined space; pay still more and you will have a 550 mm-wide super seat. All seats are covered in a fine burgundy fabric on which the project team agreed instantly, something that did not always happen. Like Feste's doublet of changeable taffeta in *Twelfth Night*, the colour alters according to the fall of light so the seating should never look uniform.

Once repairs were completed to the brickwork of the riverside wall, new metal windows, made by Crittall to replace those the company supplied in 1932, were fitted.

On 16 July 2010 and after some last-minute scampering, Mace handed the completed theatre over to the Royal Shakespeare Company. The project was on time and on budget. The RSC team marked the significant moment by swapping from white to blue hard hats; they also donned new high-visibility vests with the 'transforming our theatres' message on the back.

From the handover until the phased opening in November, Company staff settled in as lights, technical equipment and furniture were introduced and the kitchens, restaurant, bars, shop and box office were fitted out. One of the last items to be installed in the new RST was a theatrical curtain, a surprise inclusion since curtains are essential in proscenium arch theatres but redundant in those with thrust stages. But the new curtain was a grand romantic gesture dreamed up by the architects Bennetts Associates and enthusiastically endorsed by the project team.

There had been a stage curtain in the old RST, although it was seldom, if ever, seen during the last years of the theatre's life. It seems a new one was installed some time in the 1960s to the benefit of Ian Richardson, one of the RSC's greatest actors, who died in 2007 and whose ashes are buried in the theatre's foundations with a companionable bottle of whisky.

'When they replaced [the curtain], the theatre manager offered bits of it to anyone who wanted it,' said Richardson's son Miles, who played a duke, lord, knight and bishop in the 2006-08 *Histories* cycle.

'There must have been many others who had wonderful thick brown velvet curtains in their houses as we did.'

The new RST's rich red curtain, which also evokes the name of the Curtain Theatre in Shoreditch in which Shakespeare and the Lord Chamberlain's Men acted between 1597 and 1599, is nowhere near the stage. Instead, it winds around the outside wall of the auditorium and members of the audience pass through it to take their seats. It is no longer a barrier between actor and audience, but a point of entry into the shared room where theatre happens.

Before work began on the transformation of the Royal Shakespeare Theatre, Flip Tanner, the Project Coordinator, led the Company's technical working party on a trip to the Tyne Theatre in Newcastle upon Tyne.

The back of the proscenium arch seen from level three

The RST undergoes the final preparations for reopening

The Tyne, built in 1867 and still welcoming audiences 150 years later, has a beautiful, traditional proscenium auditorium hailed by The Theatres Trust as 'undoubtedly one of the finest of its date in Britain'. But the relevance of this Grade I listed theatre to the creation of a 21st century thrust stage auditorium within a building listed a mere Grade II* may not be immediately obvious.

The RSC working party, made up of the Company's experts in engineering, lighting, sound, automation and theatre design, lingered just long enough in the stalls to see the name 'Shakespeare' inscribed in a prominent place above the stage before descending beneath it to see Victorian stage machinery which, restored by theatre consultant David Wilmore in 1980 and then reconstructed after a fire in 1985, remains in working order.

The group took a professional interest in the windlasses formerly used to raise dancing Geordie lasses to the bright lights above and then asked Wilmore how far they were below the stage. 'Oh, about seven metres,' he said.

That, the group agreed, would be a desirable depth for the basement of the new RST.

The stage elevator: used mainly to transport scenery from the stores below to the stage, it can also itself be used as a scenic effect

The space comes in three levels like a wedding cake. The first, a little higher than the upper circle at 12 metres above the stage, is for the bridge from which actors, defying their vertigo, descend into the action via ropes, lifts or whatever terrifying contraption a director or designer demands. The next level, three metres higher up, is for lighting and here lighting clusters travel on tracks like an inverted railway.

The clusters evolved partly from a wish for greater flexibility but mainly from concerns for the safety of the people who have to service them. Modern theatres make increasing use of lights that can twist and swivel and can be remotely focused from a control desk. But they still need to be maintained.

The RSC's Board was not convinced. A seven-metre basement close to a river would create almost as large a hole in the budget and the technical team was urged to settle for a shallower space. After long meetings to consider compromises that were both less expensive and less expansive, the Board eventually took the plunge into the seven-metre space. 'To create a basement that deep was something we could do only while the new theatre was being built,' said Tanner. 'We could never have added it afterwards. We haven't been able to afford all the machinery we would have liked, but that can come later.

'The important thing is that we have that large space beneath the stage.'

A 'cluster slot': lights on clusters can fly in to light the stage beyond

At The Courtyard, lights were suspended below traditional bridges and familiar catwalks. To change a bulb (known in the theatre as a lamp), one of the lighting team would have to don a hard hat and safety harness, lie flat on a bridge and reach down through a trapdoor; to move a light would involve a dizzying ascent in a cherry-picker.

Holes of whatever size required – from Ophelia's grave to Malvolio's prison – can now be created on stage wherever directors want them and can remain in place throughout a season; in the old RST, Ophelia could be interred in only a limited number of places.

There is even more space – 18 metres of it – above the stage, more than enough for a couple of Bohemias or Elsinores, not to mention Illyria, Athens and a wood nearby and the entire Forest of Arden. The process of frequently changing plays and sets in a complex repertory season has become much easier.

Vince Herbert, the RSC's Head of Lighting, was convinced that it would be much safer if up to four lights were rigged on lightweight portable structures that could be independently lowered to the ground for maintenance. 'Such a system of clusters would give us much greater versatility,' he said. 'We could have a low shot, a high shot and even a tracking shot, following scenery as it flies in. We could also drop a cluster behind a window or a door without having to put a light on a stand.'

A moving light has its drawbacks: when it stops moving, the cradle from which it is suspended continues to swing for up to ten minutes while its beam moves across the focus point in a most undramatic way. Herbert assumed the technology existed to deal with the problem; when he couldn't find it, he headed for the swings in a park

in Stratford. 'My theory was that if I could start myself swinging by moving my legs one way, I could stop myself by moving my legs the other way. After that, I started playing around with a few ideas and eventually came up with a prototype. Amazingly, it worked first time. We had set ourselves the goal of stopping the structure swinging within half the normal time.

'We soon realised we could stop it swinging in under two seconds.'

Herbert's invention (one component of which comes from a child's toy) sits on top of the cluster. When it senses movement, it spins a plate in the opposite rotation and the wobble stops almost at once. This clever device, known as the RSC Lightlock, was patented and is now on commercial sale. It has since helped keep lights steady on Lady Gaga and Bon Jovi, won industry awards and become a cheerful spin-off (and a nice little earner) from the reconstruction of the RST; it was subsequently acclaimed as the 2010 Live Design Lighting Accessory of the Year.

Just under the roof lies the sophisticated engineering the theatre needs: 'It was as important to get this right as the basement,' said Tanner.

'Shakespeare was well aware of both heaven and hell in the theatre.'

Space above and below stage has added flexibility the Company has never known before. From their position close to the roof, staff can lower to the stage almost anything a designer demands: a boat, perhaps, to be shipwrecked in *The Tempest*, or Lear's storm-tossed heath. Their duty done, boat and heath can be hoisted back up to dangle safely until required again. Any item

The stage from on high, in the space where tall scenery can be flown out

of scenery not needed can be moved back to be stored in the old fly tower. Previously it had to be lugged out of the building and stored in trucks parked outside.

Manoeuvres are handled by sophisticated winches that the puniest arm can control with the help of computer software. Wires from thrones, beds or palace walls pass up through holes in a mesh floor high above the stage before doing a 90-degree turn to pass over pulleys and through acoustic walls that baffle sound to one of the 60 winches assembled by Trekwerk, the Dutch company that suffered and speedily recovered from a major fire in 2008.

There are 96 hoist points in total, possibly enough to keep Cecil B DeMille happy, and sophisticated new clutches on the winches have doubled their capacity and added still more flexibility for less cost.

As in the Swan, the RST now has an air conditioning system developed to provide silent comfort in concert halls. Air released at stalls level rises gently upwards by convection and heat. How this would impact on a single petal or leaf dropped from on high would only emerge when the first plays took to the stage.

Nicholas Edwards, an auditorium designer specialising in room acoustics, wanted to make sure that every word of those plays should be audible in the new theatre. He also wanted audiences to be aware of their own laughs or gasps from any part of the new space.

The RST job, one of the most challenging he had ever taken on, gave him sleepless nights. 'I have done many difficult spaces, including found spaces for Birmingham Opera, but at the RST the stakes were particularly high.

The yard grid: a series of catwalks serving the lighting facilities

The stage house during construction looking down into the stage elevator

The dimmer room

The 'get-in' area in the colonnade

'The RSC is such an important company and the building will define the nature of performance for that company for the next hundred years. There was no margin of error. The thrust form of the new RST is not the shape an acoustician would choose intuitively because part of the audience is always behind the performer. Our challenge was to make it actually work.'

Everyone involved with the design of the auditorium was trying to bring the audience as close as possible to the stage; but the more steeply people were stacked up, the fewer surfaces were available to reflect sound and move it behind an actor. Edwards' solution was to tilt forward the oak panels lining the drum wall by 2.5 degrees and so move the reflected sound by five degrees; the panels on the front of the stalls balcony were tilted backwards by 5.5 degrees; panels at the front of the circle were fixed upright, their edges diffracting sound in all directions.

Outside the auditorium, there was much discussion about how to get large chunks of scenery into the building. One solution was to create a new entrance on the river side of the Swan, but that would have caused complex design problems for the green room and dressing room block. So the position of the entrance used for the 'get-in' has remained unchanged: off Waterside and close to the Swan's opened-up carriage arch.

That entrance, however, is now enclosed within the new colonnade housing the box office and shop. It is a public space and those large items of scenery will have to cross it to enter the theatre through huge doors. The compromise and inconvenience are tempered by the presence of our old friends, the ghosts in the walls: this is the route by which scenery entered the theatre for more than 70 years and that tradition lives on.

Tanner lived with the reconstruction of the Royal Shakespeare Theatre for four years. He eventually concluded that builders and theatre people are not natural collaborators because they think differently: theatre people are conditioned to service plays and react to change up to the last moment.

'It's a first-night culture,' said Tanner. 'The theatre team has pushed the building team constantly to revise and finesse and to make the building perfect. But building contracts are not geared to work like that. The hardest thing proved to be taking the Royal Shakespeare Company on a different kind of journey from the one it takes to stage a play.'

But it worked: the RST was handed over on time and on budget.

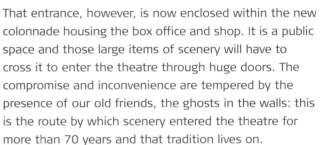

The builders' night audience

In November 2010, the RSC showed off its reconstructed theatre to journalists and the public at the end of an immensely complex reconstruction that had lasted for three and a half years.

All the world, as Richard III observed, is cheered by the sun and that week a brilliant sun shone on the RST's new cloud-capped tower during some of the coldest November days in recent weather history. If it was distinctly chilly on Monday, it was Moscow-cold by Saturday when the audience arrived for the traditional builders' night performance through foyers kitted out with auxiliary heaters.

That evening, Julian Glover, who first acted at the Shakespeare Memorial Theatre in 1957, delivered with precision and attention-grabbing intensity the prologue to *Henry V*, the same lines Samuel West had spoken at a similar event in The Courtyard four years earlier. He turned until half the audience could see only his back;

every Shakespearean word came over loud and clear.

Piece out our imperfections with your thoughts:
Into a thousand parts divide on man,
And make imaginary puissance.
Think when we talk of horses, that you see them
Printing their proud hoofs i'th'receiving earth . . .

Glover, as it happened, did not speak the first words of Shakespeare on the new stage; he was pre-empted by a small group, including Nick Asbury, who had delivered the Seven Ages of Man speech two weeks earlier at an event

24 November 2010: members of the public explore the colonnade

designed to test the theatre before it could be given its local authority licence. 'I came off stage and the first thing I said to Michael Boyd was "It works",' said Asbury. 'I came in booming and found I had to drop [the volume] down. You can finally be subtle. Not something I've ever been accused of before.'

The opening week was designed to be low-key, a chance to test the building and deal with any snags before the first play (*King Lear*) took to the stage three months later. There was no official opener, no ribbon cutting. On the first public day, 26 drama students waited for the doors to open at 9am with a clutch of *Stratford-upon-Avon Herald* readers who had come closest in a competition to guess the number of steps in the tower (174).

More than 3,300 people toured the building that day. One told Vikki Heywood that he had lived in Stratford all his life but had never been inside the RST. 'But I've had a fantastic time today and now I'm going to buy a ticket,' he said. Kathleen Thornley from Chipping Campden, which she could almost see from the top of the tower, was bowled over. 'I've been coming here since I was a child. It's been quite emotional. I could have cried with joy when I walked into the new auditorium.'

'Hugely emotional': the builders' night entertainment comes to a close

9am on 24 November 2010: the doors open to the public for the first time

The builders' night entertainment, devised by Gregory Doran and introduced by Katy Stephens and Joe Dixon, was a relaxed affair, more of a party than a pull-out-all-the-stops production. It began with a brass fanfare from Paul Englishby's music for *Coriolanus*, the last play seen in the untransformed RST, followed by John Barnard's overture (with borrowings from Thomas Arne's setting of Where the Bee Sucks from *The Tempest*), composed for the opening of the first Shakespeare Memorial Theatre in 1879.

Jane Lapotaire read John Masefield's ode written for the opening of Elisabeth Scott's theatre in 1932: 'May this house be famous. May it be the home of lovely players. May this day begin an age of gold . . .'. Poet and rapper Kate Tempest then gave a passionate performance of her Modern Day Response to the RST:

Let this be more than a theatre, let this be a space where Contemporary holds hands with Eternity, when poetry connects us with all that we are.

Speeches and party pieces followed: Project Director Peter Wilson led his own troupe of builder-dancers in a heavy-booted routine; Ian Hughes thanked every donor, contractor and anyone else he could think of in a rewrite of a Gilbert and Sullivan patter song; and Bennetts

From left: Rab Bennetts (bowler), Simon Erridge (trilby) and Alasdair McKenzie (flat cap) take to the stage

Associates did a comic turn scripted by Alasdair McKenzie and based on the John Cleese, Ronnie Barker and Ronnie Corbett classic on the English class system. 'Not being an actor, I can see why performing is so addictive,' said Rab Bennetts, who, wearing a bowler, looked down on both Simon Erridge (trilby) and McKenzie (flat cap). 'I have spoken at major conferences many times but nothing compares to standing on "our" stage at the Royal Shakespeare Theatre addressing 1,000 people.

'Puck's last speech from *A Midsummer Night's Dream* brought tears to the eyes. We never try to pre-judge the success of a building as we are too close to it, so hearing and feeling such a warm response from the people who really matter was simply thrilling.'

Susie Sainsbury also appeared on stage as part of a fun routine in which objects (including a Sainsbury's carrier bag and a very long whip) were plucked from her handbag for a supposed time capsule. 'I had never imagined I would ever be on a Stratford stage but when Greg asked me I realised I wanted to be there to be part of that night,' she said, adding that one evening a day or two earlier, she had stopped dead as she approached the RST. 'It was dark and suddenly I saw the building, not just lit as it had been for several weeks, but with people behind the glass and animated at every level. It looked

like a theatre for the first time in its entire life, a really exciting place to be.

'That was a hugely emotional moment.'

It took Vikki Heywood a few weeks to fathom her own response. 'It felt exactly as it does about four weeks after you have brought your first baby back from hospital. You realise that everything is going to be different from now on. I don't think I had realised just how much this building was going to bring about a positive change for the Company and its relationship with its audience. We could not turn the clock back.'

In the weeks leading up to the RST's reopening Sir Christopher Bland had regularly walked with five or so others in the 'empty and somewhat echoing' theatre. 'The difference between an auditorium of 1,040 empty seats and one full of eager, expectant faces is quite transforming. It feels right. You choose colours, you choose lavatories, you choose seats, you choose a configuration for the thrust stage. But we couldn't know how the theatre would work until it was full of people –

The transformed Royal Shakespeare Theatre at dusk

and we couldn't really know how it would work until the Shakespeare plays, for which it had been designed, began to be performed.'

The media days that had begun the week were distinguished by the spectacularly varied chairs, plucked from the Company's furniture store, on which the RSC great and good sat, not entirely comfortably, on stage to answer questions. Michael Boyd did not sit still for long, preferring to prowl up and down, left to right, to show off his new auditorium's acoustics and prove that **he could be heard by those to whom he had turned his back as he whispered to those he faced.**

The media response varied. 'Great things deserve to happen here, and great Shakespearean speeches given,' enthused Jonathan Glancey in *The Guardian*. 'And now you'll even be able to hear them from the cheap seats.' Charles Spencer told his *Daily Telegraph* readers: 'For the first time the RSC's home base seems genuinely welcoming and the juxtaposition of weathered bricks with modern steel and plate glass, strikes me as truly dramatic.' But Tom Dyckhoff in *The Times* suggested he would find 'more drama, intrigue, seduction and surprise in Watford Gap services'. It takes all sorts.

As journalists and public wandered through the building, members of the 2009-11 ensemble were waiting in the wings, desperate to play in the new auditorium but knowing their cues would not come until the following February. 'Many signed up for the ensemble because they wanted to do a play there,' said Noma Dumezweni. 'At a meeting in 2010 we were told that, because of the way the schedule had been prepared, nine people would not get to play on the main stage. To a man and woman everyone said, "No way. That cannot happen. You have to change the schedule". And it didn't happen.

The foyer and relic wall

They made it work. We said that we had signed up to be part of the new RST. We wanted to be part of history.'

The actors wanted to know how the new RST would compare with The Courtyard, which for many had been their first experience of a thrust stage; they had liked it – once they got the hang of it. 'When you stand centre stage, you look round a room full of faces,' said Jonathan Slinger, a formidable Richard III. 'You can see everyone and you are immediately able to contact them very easily in one sweep. Shakespeare was writing with audience engagement in mind and unless you have that engagement you are doing his works a disservice.'

Forbes Masson added that, with Shakespeare, the audience was 'part of the beast. I think we really found that in The Courtyard. I always think the audience is like another character in the production. You can really feel their energy. With the force of the audience on all sides, it just feels much more energising. There is no place to hide.'

At times an actor might feel the need to project forcefully; at other times the big voice was not needed. 'As Friar Laurence, I had a scene at the end of *Romeo and Juliet* in which I had to list what had happened in the play. I found I could bring it really low and not do very much. As a space, it could be so small, so intimate.'

Chuk Iwuji had a similar experience as Henry VI. 'When I did the molehill speech, I just sat in the middle of the stage and felt easily able to see and communicate with everyone and reach out to them with only the slightest turn. Very often reactions came out of being able to see people's faces very clearly. You are so visible. When you have that kind of communion, that's when really exciting things happen.'

Old RSC hands were also impressed. Sir Ian McKellen,

Taking in the new
auditorium as projections
from past RSC
performances are beamed
onto the proscenium arch

who had played Lear and Sorin in *The Seagull* in The
Courtyard, summed up how the auditorium would be
judged: 'If in the new RST the audience can hear more
easily and see the actors' faces more easily, then it will
be a winner and that will be an improvement over the
theatre it has replaced.'

Sir Patrick Stewart, Claudius in Doran's production of
Hamlet, had worked on the rather different thrust stage
at the Guthrie Theater in Minneapolis and found the
experience challenging. 'But once I was familiar with it,
I loved it. When I first walked into The Courtyard to see
a production of one of Michael Boyd's *Henry VI* plays, I
was excited by the proximity of the stage to the audience
and in anticipation of how the director would use the stage.

'But I wondered what happened when you came to a
soliloquy. In a proscenium theatre, you have only one
audience to think about, to share your thoughts with.
In a thrust, you could say you have three audiences and
I thought that was going to present difficulties. In fact,
it was quite the opposite. In the king's prayer in *Hamlet*,
I found that I could truthfully speak those lines aloud,
make them naturalistic and spontaneous and easily share
the content of the speech and the emotion of the
character with the entire theatre.'

As the theatre opened, news began to leak of his debut
in the reshaped RST: he would play Shylock in *The
Merchant of Venice* in 2011, one of the first new
productions for the new stage.

The restored riverside wall

View from the stage:
the new auditorium seen
from upstage centre

Two days after the big glass doors of the new Royal Shakespeare Theatre slid open to the public for the first time, Michael Boyd said he and his RSC colleagues felt massively relieved, hugely proud and vindicated. But they would not be uncorking the champagne (or, more likely in an era of arts cuts, fizzy mineral water), not least because the Company was about to open both a season in London and a Christmas show in Stratford.

'All of us feel we are still in the storm so we can't party yet, really smile yet. The embodiment of relief and jubilation will probably come later.'

At that moment, a short but spectacular barrage of fireworks, including a monsoon of Golden Rain and the pyrotechnic equivalent of a 21-gun salute, filled the Warwickshire night and halted all conversation.

'The sky is rebuking me for failing to celebrate,'

observed Boyd as the display, marking the switch-on of Stratford's Christmas lights, faded away.

19

A couple of months later, he was more ready to engage in some understated jubilation about the rebirth of his theatre. 'It's better than I thought it would be. I had thought something was bound to be not quite right. Perhaps the colonnade or the Swan bar or the Scott bar would not work. But all the spaces have proved to be fine. I had been more certain about the auditorium; I didn't think we would get that wrong because we had the extraordinary privilege of being able to try out The Courtyard for a year before we signed off the design.'

But his special RST moment of revelation and reassurance was as exciting as it was unexpected;

it came early in January 2011 as the amateurs of the Stratford Musical Theatre Company presented a one-off performance of their production of *Return to the Forbidden Planet*, the musical inspired by *The Tempest*.

Peter Brook, veteran director and author of one of the most significant books on the nature of theatre, had

Waiting in the wings of the new RST

The glass frontage linking the tower to the rest of the building

been in Stratford to present *Love Is My Sin*, his arrangement of 31 Shakespeare sonnets as a dramatic narrative, in the Swan. On the *Forbidden Planet* day, his assistant had told Boyd that Brook's ideas for his theatre at the Bouffes du Nord in Paris had been inspired by a painting in which a wall of faces tipped forward into the empty space of an auditorium. 'That night, with the house full for *Forbidden Planet*, I looked across the auditorium, saw a wall of eager faces and immediately imagined the picture Peter had seen,' said Boyd.

As the show began, people in the audience were urged to do various silly things to get the spaceship to fly – raise their hands in the air, wiggle fingers, pat heads. 'A woman next to me said to the man she was with, "If only we could see ourselves". I told her we could – we were looking at people directly across the theatre doing identical things. We were copying each other, in touch with each other. I knew we had been right not to go for some big, wide "flexible space", nor for the sacred Greek arena of the Olivier, Chichester or the Crucible in Sheffield.'

That night in the RST would have been sufficient reason to reach for the fireworks, light the blue touch paper and send a joyous rocket into the Stratford sky. But there were other reasons to celebrate. Following a deal with the Roundhouse announced in December 2010, the Company's place in London was assured for five years in a space it liked well. And down the road at The Courtyard, *Matilda*, a musical version of Roald Dahl's novel, had proved to be a huge hit with both public and critics.

The energy and exuberance of the production (not to mention three casts of irrepressible children) was both a triumphant affirmation of the success of The Courtyard and an auspicious omen for the creative potential of the thrust stage in the RST. It had also reaffirmed Boyd's faith that artistic innovation can bring box office success to the RSC at a time of reduced support from the public

Foyer space across different levels of the transformed theatre

The tower rising above the Swan Theatre entrance

purse. 'There is a pragmatic aspect to that because one thing that will be a priority for us over the next five years will be an emphasis on revenue earning.'

The future of The Courtyard itself was still uncertain at this stage. It had been conceived as a temporary building, had been granted planning permission despite strenuous opposition from some Stratford residents and should have been removed by 31 March 2010. The mood had changed, however, and the RSC sought and won an extension until the end of 2012 so that The Courtyard could play its part in the World Shakespeare Festival, due to take place during the Cultural Olympiad. There was even a polite clamour for the building to become a permanent fixture, which might suit the Company as it sought to regain the kind of experimental space provided by the first and second versions of The Other Place.

'The cheapest and quickest way might be to take away the auditorium interior of The Courtyard and replace it with a small studio box theatre inside the rusty shed. But we may not get permission to keep it.' (If the planners were to say no, Boyd had fantasised about hiring a Chinook helicopter to pick up the building and whisk it away to some perfect site in London.)

Other more certain aspects of the future were looking bright and Boyd felt confident enough to look ahead to things to come, both actual and potential, including his then imminent *Macbeth*, the first production of a Shakespeare play made for the new auditorium. ('I think the new RST has qualities that will serve that play well.') The completion of the rebuild had also prompted him to ponder not just witches, ghosts and daggers but also the future of the RSC, the nature of Shakespeare performance and the role of theatre in society.

He offered some predictions. One was that the RSC ensemble could develop from a large company of actors

working with a very varied list of directors into a smaller and tighter band led by a single creative team. 'We may explore drilling deeper in a smaller hole with a smaller team over a period of time and see where that takes us in terms of virtuosity, expressive power, depth.'

The World Shakespeare Festival might also prove to be a significant engine for change at the RSC. 'We will bring the most inspiring pieces of theatre work here from around the world and ask ourselves how we measure up, how we can develop our practice by learning from best practice elsewhere.'

As the RSC moved into its second half-century, it would honour the great traditions set by Sir Peter Hall and later artistic directors but also explore other traditions and develop its interest in theatre that spilled through space in three dimensions; the two were not mutually exclusive. 'For much of my career, I have sensed a quiet civil war in British theatre between a literary, scholarly, text-based tradition and a more European, performance-orientated, and embodied approach to theatre-making. I just don't buy into that civil war. I have consistently refused to accept (for instance) that textual coherence and narrative need be the enemy of vivid expressive theatre.

'Much has happened in terms of movement and performance since the RSC was founded in 1961 and our visual senses are more sophisticated, more able to edit words and images rapidly. We have the option to use a shallow, almost end-on thrust in the new auditorium but we have chosen to open the theatre with its fullest thrust, not only because it brings the house closer to the stage but because there are more people frustrated and bored by inappropriately static and text-bound theatre than there are people frustrated by intermittently seeing the back of an actor as part of a dialogue on a thrust stage. Audiences want kinetic as well as literary satisfaction.

The Scott bar, with retained Art Deco features

Transformed: the Royal Shakespeare Theatre

'I don't accept that the embodied, total theatre which is encouraged by a thrust stage means bad scripts or bad verse speaking or illiteracy on the part of theatre. In Shakespeare's own time, dance, song, and virtuoso sword fighting were under-written in his scripts but understood to be integral to performance.'

Boyd's explanation of how he wanted to use the three-dimensional space in the RST began to sound startlingly similar to the way the medieval creator of a doom painting might describe how he used the two-dimensional space above the chancel of a church. 'We have to try to find meaning in the sculptural significance of a staging, to employ an understanding of social space, erotic space, the politics of power and movement through space.'

His amateur's interest in neuroscience had led him into an examination of the relationship between theatre space and the brain of the actor as he or she stands on the new stage between theatrical heaven above and hell below. He also regretted the decline of the habit of contemplative congregation. 'Church attendances are

Foyer space between the drum wall of the auditorium and the 1932 relic wall

falling and we now have too few opportunities to gather and share our thoughts as a community. If theatre is to thrive, it must celebrate its own distinct capacities and gifts. No other art form enables and requires the witnessing and participation in the full human presence as theatre does, and no theatre maker more than Shakespeare. This new theatre will allow a large audience to share his ideas and his great emotions in the full human presence of each other and the performers, over real time, sharing the same space, and breathing the same air.

'A "community for the night" can here share those big questions:

how can we live together without hurting each other? How do you cope with falling in love? What does ecstatic happiness really feel like? And how do you live with the certain knowledge that you are going to die when you can also dream of immortality?'

That sense of community and connection was what Boyd felt at the performance of *Return to the Forbidden Planet*, even if that show did not attempt to suggest answers to his big questions. And no answers will be attempted here, for this is the end of the last chapter of the book about the Transformation project. The questions must be passed on to actors, directors, designers and Shakespeare himself to explore on the big new stage between heaven and hell. The Transformation story has not ended; the reopening of the RST marks only the end of the beginning. Appropriately for a theatre whose new life began with *Macbeth*, the story will continue

tomorrow and tomorrow and tomorrow . . .

Afterword

So this part of the history of the Royal Shakespeare Company draws to a close. Now the artists and audiences will come together to create the performances of the future within the new building.

If we open the new Royal Shakespeare Theatre with confidence, it is partly because we have had the unprecedented privilege of nearly five years of practice in The Courtyard Theatre. Serving as both our wonderful temporary home and as a prototype, it has not only taught us invaluable lessons which we have applied to the RST, but also given ample evidence that this unique thrust space can be the fertile home of unmatchable theatrical experiences.

Our best assumptions will be subverted nonetheless: the new theatre will be used in ways we haven't imagined, and the walls will grow new scars, new badges of the courage and achievements of another generation.

As we watch audiences come into the building for the first time we are already excited by the opportunities it gives the RSC. This is a theatre that welcomes people from all ages and all walks of life. It invites you to explore old and new connections with Shakespeare and the contemporary performance of his work. It is a sociable place which allows you to make a human connection with both the artists onstage and with each other as an audience.

Thank you to all who worked so hard to make it happen and shared our vision with such insight and skill.

Michael Boyd and **Vikki Heywood**

Acknowledgements

Writing this book has been hugely enjoyable. My thanks are due to everyone who agreed to be interviewed and endured repeated questions when I failed to grasp things first time around. I apologise for the inevitable omissions, especially to any otters who feel I should have found space to describe the new holt built for them on the Avon as part of the Transformation project.

The RSC's Kevin Wright has been an admirably calm and reassuring supporter. Sally Brambles, the assiduous copy editor, has pored over the words and found many clangers. My friends Kim Bishop, Mick Wilkins, Nigel Westbrook (the hyphen tsar) and Michael Smith have all read the text and made valuable suggestions.

I am indebted to Marian Pringle for her generosity in letting me borrow so much from her authoritative *The Theatres of Stratford-upon-Avon, 1875-1992: An Architectural History* and for reading and correcting Chapter 2. Mrs Pringle died in December 2010, just after the RST, about which she knew so much, opened to the public.

I am grateful to Patric Gilchrist and staff at Theatre by the Lake in Keswick, Cumbria, for hiring me and then for commissioning a book on TBTL's first ten years: it showed me how to do this one.

During long days in the shed, my grandchildren, Ailis, Maeve and Ned, have never been far from my mind and I hope they will come to enjoy many happy nights in the transformed Royal Shakespeare Theatre.

My wife Pauline, who first came to the RST as a child, has encouraged and cajoled me and read the text at every stage; she probably knows it as well as she knows *Macbeth*. She has also run the show. I hope she knows how grateful I am.

David Ward
The Hut
Bollington
January 2011

Facts and Figures

An average of 125 people per day worked on the site

The furthest seat is 15 metres from the RST stage; in the 1932 theatre it was 27 metres

Around 1 million hours were worked on site

5,000 reclaimed bricks were used

168,000 new bricks were handmade, including 14,000 'special bricks'

The RST stage is 24.5 metres long – of which 10.25 metres is thrust (in front of the original proscenium arch) and 14.25 metres is original stage within the fly tower – by 7.2 metres wide

The Swan Theatre stage is 13 metres long – of which 10.5 metres is thrust – by 5.8 metres wide

The Courtyard Theatre stage is 16.9 metres long – of which 10.51 metres is thrust (in front of the false proscenium) – by 7.4 metres wide

1,046 seats in the RST, plus 14 standing: 502 in the stalls yard and rear stalls; 266 in the circle; 278 in the upper circle. 22 seats fold into the floor to create 6 wheelchair positions in the rear stalls, 4 in the circle and 2 in the upper circle. There are 24 different seat types over 4 levels

429 seats in the Swan Theatre, plus 32 standing

The RST stage house grid (fly tower) is 19 metres high with 15 metres' flying space above the stage

People from over 80 countries contributed to the Transforming Our Theatres Appeal

18,000 people visited the theatre during its first week of opening

Overstage Engineering System

There are 60 dual winches which provide up to 120 flexibly deployable motorised points for the suspension of technical equipment and movement of scenic elements, including performer flying

Each dual winch is capable of lifting a payload of 400 kilograms

The modular dual winches can be located in any of 104 potential locations above the thrust and endstage

There are 30 lighting clusters arranged over and around the thrust stage which can each support a payload of 120 kilograms and can be flexibly deployed into over 53 positions

The overstage system features regenerative technology which can store energy used for downward motions to assist in upward movements, reducing the overall energy required for the system

Understage Engineering System

In the order of 100 tonnes of steelwork was used in the construction of the structural frame for the stage

The steelwork for the stage structure was erected in 3 weeks and involved the use of 4 mini-cranes and 10 motorised work platforms

The scenic lift set within the stage floor is capable of moving a load of 10 tonnes at a speed of 2 metres per second

When locked into position, the scenic lift can support a distributed load of 56 tonnes

The stage floor features around 150 modular panels that can be removed to form voids and allow for the positioning of trapdoors and lifts

Stage Lighting and Audiovisual Systems

355 miles (572 kilometres) of cabling was installed as part of the stage lighting and audiovisual infrastructure

There are 423 facilities panels within the building providing wired services for the stage lighting and audiovisual infrastructure

Over 40 individual loudspeakers make up the sound-reinforcement system within the RST

Design and Project Team

Architects Bennetts Associates
Engineers Buro Happold
Theatre Consultants Charcoalblue
Acoustic Engineers Acoustic Dimensions
Cost Consultants Gardiner & Theobald
Project Management and Strategic Planning Drivers Jonas Deloitte
Construction Managers Mace

Trade Contractors

Hewden Stuart Plc, Wingate Electrical PLC, Select Plant Hire Company Ltd, Taylor's Hoists, Sky Scaffolding (Midlands) Ltd, Site Engineering Services Ltd, Elliott Thomas Ltd, DSM Demolition Limited, Cementation Foundations Skanska, John Doyle, Billington Structural Steelwork, Deepdale Solutions Limited, Crittall Windows, Varla (UK) Limited, M&J Roofing, Lesterose, Fireclad, Shaylor Special Projects, Szerelmey, Loughton, Swift Horsman, Taylor Made Joinery, KLH UK Limited, Glazzard, CMF, S Lucas, G F Tomlinson Birmingham Ltd, Poltrona Frau, Rotary North West Limited, Ductwork Wolverhampton Limited, AES Limited, Michael J Lonsdale, Stage Electrics, ThyssenKrupp Elevator UK Limited, Delstar Engineering, Trekwerk BV, Niscayah, Fitzgerald Contractors Limited, Hasmead Limited

Fit-Out Contractors

AMC Contracts (UK) Ltd, Court Catering Equipment Ltd, DMA Signs Ltd

INTERNATIONAL COUNCIL

In order to raise the profile of the RSC and its transformation internationally, a leading group of artists, philanthropists and advocates established the RSC International Council. The Company is delighted to recognise this important group.

Dame Judi Dench DBE *Honorary Chair*
Lady Sainsbury of Turville CBE *Chair*

Sir Eric and Lady Anderson
Frances Barber
Sir Christopher and Lady Bland
Lee C. Bollinger
Michael Boyd
David and Sandra Burbidge
Michael and Susan Clasper
Michael and Felicia Crystal
Miranda Curtis
Sinead Cusack
Gregory Doran
Mark and Sandy Foster
Tony and Linda Hales
Sir Peter Hall CBE
Charlotte Heber Percy
Vikki Heywood
Michael and Mercedes Hoffman
The Rt Hon Lord and Lady Iliffe
Laurence Isaacson CBE
Sir Derek Jacobi CBE
Tussi Kluge
Bruce and Suzie Kovner
Nick and Alyssa Lovegrove
Jon and Lillian Lovelace
Sir Ian McKellen CBE RA
Doug and Julie McPherson
Alexander Patrick DL and Valerie Patrick
Mark Pigott OBE
Ian Ritchie CBE RA and
   Jocelyne van den Bossche
Royal Shakespeare Theatre Trust
Sir Antony Sher KBE
Jonathan Slinger
Raymond and Phyllis Smith
Sir Patrick Stewart OBE
Stratford-upon-Avon Town Trust
David Suchet CBE
Peter and Nancy Thompson
Mary Weston CBE
Leslie and Abigail Wexner

In memory of the late Elnora Ferguson and John Kluge, founding members of the International Council

We are immensely grateful to everyone who has supported the transformation of the Royal Shakespeare Company's theatres in Stratford-upon-Avon, including all those donors who wish to remain anonymous. In particular we would like to thank:

Public funders
Supported by the National Lottery
   through Arts Council England
Advantage West Midlands

Private funders
29th May 1961 Charitable Trust
Marie Alexander
The Anson Charitable Trust
Jeffrey and Mary Archer
John Ballantine
Neil and Ann Benson
Lord and Lady Bhattacharyya
Simon C Blakey
Sir Christopher and Lady Bland
Lord & Lady Blyth of Rowington
David and Sandra Burbidge
CHK Charities Limited
Michael and Susan Clasper
The John S Cohen Foundation
Michael and Felicia Crystal
Miranda Curtis
Felix Dennis
Jane and Howard Epstein*
The Eranda Foundation
Allan & Nesta Ferguson Charitable Trust
Mort and Frannie Fleishhacker*
Mark and Sandy Foster
The Foundation for Sport and the Arts
The Foyle Foundation
The Gatsby Charitable Foundation
J Paul Getty Jnr Charitable Trust
Mr David Grove OBE and Mrs Jane Grove
Ros and Alan Haigh
Tony and Linda Hales
Christine Hands
Mercedes and Michael Hoffman*
The Iliffe Family Charitable Trust
Laurence Isaacson CBE*
Clive Jones and Vikki Heywood
The Florence Amelia Kendrew Charitable
   Trust
Jonathan and Deborah Kestenbaum
The Kresge Foundation
The John W Kluge Foundation*
Land Securities
Richard Pasco CBE and Barbara Leigh-Hunt
The Limoges Trust
LJC Fund
Nick and Alyssa Lovegrove*
Jon and Lillian Lovelace*

Doug and Julie McPherson*
Paul and Shirlie Morrell
Catherine and Kenneth Mountney
Dr Barbara Oldham
PACCAR Foundation
The Patrick Trust
PF Charitable Trust
The Pragnell Family
The Rigby Foundation
The Sir John Ritblat Family Foundation
Simon and Virginia Robertson
The Rockefeller Foundation*
Royal Shakespeare Theatre Trust
RSC Friends
Susie Sainsbury
The Saintbury Trust
The Schroder Foundation
The Shubert Organization*
Raymond W. and Phyllis L. Smith*
Fiona Stockwell
Stratford-upon-Avon Town Trust
Liam and Jackie Strong
Peter and Nancy Thompson
The Tolkien Trust
Constance Travis Charitable Trust
Sir Siegmund Warburg's Voluntary
   Settlement
Garfield Weston Foundation
Mary Weston Foundation
Leslie and Abigail Wexner*
HDH Wills 1965 Charitable Trust
The Wolfson Foundation

* Supporters of RSC America Inc

Take Your Seat
We are enormously grateful to all those who named a seat in the RST auditorium. The following inscriptions appear on the seats in the theatre.

2 September 2010 Jürgen Lauterbach
   and Ute Mügge-Lauterbach
50 years of pleasure Elizabeth Law
A. L. Kennedy
Ada Rehan
Adrian Terry
Alan and Jean Gayton Trust
Alan Haigh
Alan Howard
Alexander and Matthew Foster
Alexander and Nicander White
Algernon Posgate
Alice and Helen Johnson
Alice Ellen Pyle Mather
All donors to the Transforming Our
   Theatres Appeal
Allan and Judy Bell

Always say please and always say
   thank you, Ms C Jones
Andrea and Ian Bucknell and Eth Short
Andrea Kerbaker
Andrea Smith
Andrew and Ann Sharp
Andrew Michael Pettipher
Andrew Wall
Andrew, Linda, Oscar and Louis Jamieson
Andy and Karen Raynor
Angela Baddeley - donor
   Dr John B Hanson-Low
Angela Sommers Morton Andrew
   Alex Ralph and Charles
Ann and David Brierley
Ann and Roy Clark
Ann Maria Clark
Ann, David and Richard Gee
Anna and Cliff Narbett in honour
   of Alan Badel and Fabia Drake
Anne and Edward Hazel
Anne and John Peniket
Anne Brisk Ehrhardt
Annie and Grace Jones
Anonymous donors
Anthea Keir Lunt
Anthony Quayle – donor IBM United
   Kingdom Limited
Arts Educational Schools, London
Atomies
Audrey Haw
Barbara and Ken Follett
Barbara and Robert Woodthorpe Browne
Barbara Randall
Barbara Scott and Anne Milner
Barbara Young and Margaret Utridge
   - Dearest Friends
Ben Crystal
Ben, Caroline, Max and Albie Mackintosh
Bertha Rayner
Betty Percival
Bill and Cylla Dugdale
Bill and Doreen Mapleson
Bill Macbean
Bill Riddall "my legs can keep no pace
   with my desires"
Bill Shea 1926-2009 this was his paradise
Bob Alexander QC
Bob and Trish Baker
Brewster Mason
Brewster Mason – donor Tomoo Hirooka,
   President Asahi Newspapers, Japan
Brian and Phyllida Scott
Brian and Sheila Morris
Brian Cox and Nicole Ansari
Brian James Burke
Brian Kennett
Brian Mares
Broughton Castle

Campion, Lucy, Jenny (all née Graham)
Captain Peter Barnett
  and Mrs Sandra Billinge
Carla Vasa-Richardson
Caro Wilson
Carol Ann Evans
Carole Taylor and Bernice Humphreys
Caroline Stanford
Carolyn Carter Starr
Casper Hales and Crab - loyal friends
Catherine Smith - 'Out vile jelly'
Cécile Burton
Ceri Ann Roberts
Charles Kemble
Charles Twigger
Charlotte and Helena King
Charlotte Cushman
Cherry and Martin Stephenson and Family
Chris and Clem Martin
Chris Holland
Christine Knapman
Christopher Thor Nosbod
Claire Van Zant
Clara Eliza Tree
Clare and Ian Maurice
Clive and Annie Snowdon
Clive and Sylvia Richards
Clive Jones
Colin Arthur Stanley 1937-2001
Colin, Trish and Jonathan Cooper
Crissie and Andrew Milne
Cunningham family, Manchester, Durham,
  York and Leicester
Cynthia R Coatts
Cyril Turner
Dame Edith Evans - donor Tarmac Limited
Dame Peggy Ashcroft
Dame Peggy Ashcroft -
  donor Lord and Lady Gibson
Dame Sybil Thorndike -
  donor The John Lewis Partnership
Damien Tomlinson "To be or not to be"
Daniel R Baker
David and Beryl Overton
David and Judith Smith
David and Kathleen Mary Holmes
David and Pam Harrison
David and Sue Hall-Smith
David Antony Scruton. To celebrate
  60 years at the RSC
David Garrick
David Grove
David Lanch
David Sainsbury
David Stanford
David Tennant
Declan and Julie O'Brien
Denise Creamer and Tom Gill
Denne Gilkes

Derek Rudd
Des and Jean Gamlen and Family
Diana W. Mineck
Dianne Lowther
Dick Macaulay
Donald Sinden - donor The American
  Friends of the RST inc. through the
  generosity of Benjamin Ira Gertz in loving
  memory of his father Louis Simon Gertz
Doreen (Howell) Alexander 1922 - 1998
Dorothy Barlow
Dorothy Tutin - donor Donald Albery
Dorothy, Geoff and Joy Redfern,
  Maggie Simmonds
Dorothy, June and Dick Dodsworth
Doug and Julie McPherson, in honor
  of Bobby Vagt
Dr Lee Jackson, Perth, Western Australia
Dr Ranald Wishart-Dykes and
  Kenneth Wilson-Oldridge
Dr. Gordon W. Bennett, educator
Dr. Marjorie M. Fisher
Dr. Trevor A. Miles
E Wolram and R C J Len
E. and E. Wells
E. Louise Robertshaw
Edith and Andrew Seth
Edith Wynne Matthison
Edmund Kean
Edwin Booth
Edwin Forrest
Eleanor Grace Jackson. A small start to
  your theatre career! Love Mum and Dad
Elizabeth R Clarke
Elizabeth Spriggs - donor
  Contributors in Japan
Ellen Terry
Emrys James - donor Contributors in Japan
Eric and Frances Hodgess Roper
Eric and Poppy Anderson
Eugenio Miguel Sanchez
Family of Marianne Joy Naidoo-Kai.
  She loved being here
Fiona Stockwell
Fleur Bradley
Florence Amelia Kendrew
For Chris Marshall on her 60th birthday -
  8 November 2008
For Mary Dorothy Tatlow -
  WS was always the other man
For my sister Olive who taught me
  to love the theatre
For Rosemary Ingham
  from her grandchildren
For Ruth Vida Christie Yarwood 1907-2003
  who loved plays in this theatre
Frank Benson
Frank Cochrane - In affectionate memory
  from his daughters Ann, Pam and Prim

Frank Ogden
Frank R. Benson (the lesser) and Gwenyth
Freda Radcliffe - together with Norman
Frida Lee
Friedhoff and Davidson Families
G R and L A Jones
Gale and Mike Kesseler in honour of
  Charles Kay and Susan Fleetwood
Garry Weston
Gemma Kate Allred and Paul Taker
Geoffrey Littman
Geoffrey Osborne
Geoffrey Purnell 1927-1982
George and Jenny Harrison
George Anson
George Devine - donor Tony Richardson
Gill and Mike Hicks
Gill Carrick
Gill Henry and Family
Gillian Mary Laws
Gillian Wallace
Gilly Read and Monica Hastings
Glenda Jackson -
  donor Sir William E Butlin MBE
Gorsky Family
Grace Wildgoose. One other gaudy night.
  Thane Whetstone
Gregory Doran & Sir Antony Sher KBE
Greta and Peter Meredith
Guy Woolfenden
H Henderson
H.R.H. The Prince of Wales
Hannah Irene Fickus
Harry and Jack Jones
Harry Longrigg
Hazel Mary Richards 1942 - 2002
  "the last of many visits to the RSC,
  with Kelvyn"
Helen Bonfils - donor Donald Seawell
Helen Faucit
Henry Irving
Henry Lafferty
Herbert and Lilian Barton
Hilary Taylor and family
Hotchkiss School
Hugh Mellor
Ian and Anne Crichton
Imogen Beecroft
In loving memory
  Elizabeth (Betty) Leigh-Hunt
In loving memory of
  Barbara and Norman Clift
In loving memory of Dr Barbara Oldham
In loving memory of Fordham and Hersey
  Flower. For their lifelong commitment to
  the Royal Shakespeare Theatre, formerly
  the Shakespeare Memorial Theatre
In loving memory of Ivy Wride
In loving memory of Jean Stacey 1938-2007

In loving memory of John William Smith
In loving memory of Joy Bourdillon
  1912-2009
In loving memory of
  Norma and John Henfrey
In memory of Abraham Kramer
In memory of Abraham Solomon
In memory of Alan and Nancy Carver
In memory of Alan Townsend Actor
  RSC 1951-3
In memory of Albert and Myra Pearson
In memory of Albert Dyson
In memory of Alice and Bertram Castle
In memory of Andrew Winckler
In memory of
  Ann and Trevor Timperley DFC FRSA
In memory of Anne Dollar
In memory of Anne Johnson (Wilko)
  beloved of family and Hunmanby Friends
In memory of Arthur Edwards,
  Life-long member
In memory of Arthur Prandle
In memory of Bea Broad née Baker, Mummy
In memory of Bill and Kathleen Hoskins
In memory of Brewster Mason
In memory of C.R. 'John' Mullings
In memory of Carol Gorringe
In memory of Caroline Bonella
In memory of
  Catherine and Kenneth Mountney
In memory of Cecil James Rydings
In memory of Charles and Dorothy Mata
In memory of Christine Hands
In memory of Cicely M Fothergill
In memory of David A. Barrett
In memory of David A. Richardson
In memory of David Butler
In memory of David Clifford Merchant
In memory of Derek J Farmer
In memory of Derek Southion
In memory of Dick Hains
In memory of Dilys Hamlett
  RSC 1955, '56 and '98
In memory of Dixon and Amélie Boyd
In memory of Doreen Lillian Jones née Fern
In memory of Doreen Norris
In memory of Dorothy Kramer
In memory of Douglas Birch
In memory of Dr R. W. Temple
In memory of Edith and Herman Barr
In memory of Enid Cousins
In memory of Eric Pearson 1915-2006
In memory of Ernie Watts
In memory of Evadne Lloyd née Flower
In memory of Florence Watts
In memory of Frederick William Whitehead
In memory of Garry Roberts
In memory of George Hamilton Turner
In memory of George Waddell

In memory of Gladys and Joan Goss
In memory of Gladys Richards
In memory of Glyn Holroyd
In memory of Grizel Robarts
In memory of Gwen Oliver
In memory of Heather Christine Docking
In memory of Henry Gilbert Orme
 1920-2007
In memory of Hilda Wiseman
In memory of Iain Robert Pettigrew
In memory of Ian Lee 1942-2008
 "who loved the theatre"
In memory of Ian Richardson. Actor.
 1934 - 2007
In memory of Ian Stockwell
In memory of Jack Carey
In memory of Jack Gillions 1922-1970
In memory of James A. Dobbs
In memory of Jamie Cormack 1972 - 1991
In memory of Janice Pickles
In memory of Jean Chennell
In memory of Jean Glover
In memory of Jean Humphries 1927 - 2009
In memory of Jennifer Anne Brown
In memory of Jim Manley
In memory of Joan and Philip Livesey
In memory of Joan Douglas Harris
In memory of Joan Jarvis
In memory of Joan Miller
In memory of John and Mary Ball
In memory of John Ballantine
In memory of John Bright
In memory of John Burnett
In memory of John Gate
In memory of John Howard Hayes
In memory of John Rodney Cove-Smith
In memory of John V Watts
In memory of Kate Flint:
 an unforgettable teacher
In memory of Kathleen Fraser
In memory of Katreen Lack 1912-2009
In memory of Ken Jones
In memory of Kenneth Southgate,
 1927-2001
In memory of Lawrence Gordon Smith
In memory of Leslie Francis Gillett J.P.
In memory of Lionel Hunt
In memory of
 Margaret and Arthur Wellicome
In memory of Margaret and Wilbert Awdry
In memory of Margaret Doncaster née Peile
In memory of Margaret Hanson -
 "Mags" 1933 - 2009
In memory of Margaret Harris
In memory of Margaret L L McDonald
In memory of Margaret Lines
In memory of Margaret Phalp
In memory of Margaret Shinton

In memory of Marian Page who gave
 me my joy of drama. Phyllis Smith
In memory of Mary Carroll Glasnevin
In memory of Mary Joan Townsend
 1909-2008
In memory of Maurice A. Hopkins
In memory of Mick Downing from his
 many friends
In memory of Mike Davis 1962-2006
In memory of Mimi
In memory of Mr and Mrs Herbert Bolton.
 From their grandchildren, Nigel, Alistair
 and Kirsten Cairns
In memory of Mrs Mary Cromey
In memory of
 Muir Hunter QC (Hon. Gov. RSC)
In memory of Nan and Leslie Watkins
In memory of Nicki and Terry Thomas
In memory of Nora Mary Parker
 (née Salt) 1921-2008
In memory of our beautiful
 Beccy Taylor 1990-2008
In memory of P. E. V. McCarthy
In memory of Pamela Ann Mather
In memory of Patricia Healy Hamlet Act V
 Sc II Line 360
In memory of Patricia Zich
In memory of Patsy Flynn
In memory of Paul and Pauline Griffith
In memory of Penny Brindley
In memory of Pepe
In memory of Peter B Thorne
In memory of Peter Charles Howe
In memory of Pip Foulsham and
 Karl Fitzgerald
In memory of Pippa Donald
In memory of Professor Edward O. Lutz
In memory of R F Henderson
In memory of Raymond William Dallaway
In memory of Renee and Alan Jepson
In memory of Richard and Elise Allen
In memory of Richard H Tester
In memory of Robert and Rose Lovegrove
In memory of Robert Shaw b.1927 - d.1978
In memory of Robert Wolfgang Cahn
In memory of Robin Philip McKelvie
In memory of
 Roger Frank Christopher Musgrave
In memory of Roger Jones
 60's RSC Actor, A Creative Life
In memory of Ronald and Betty Bryer
In memory of Rose and Harry Davis
In memory of Rosemary Bignell
In memory of Roy Seammen
In memory of Russell Greening
 "Some are Born Great"
In memory of Ruth Adler, née Oppenheimer
In memory of Sara Clarke
In memory of Sheila Mack

In memory of Sheila Thompson
 and Nora Finch
In memory of Sheilah Warner
In memory of Shelagh Brettell
In memory of Shirley Watkins
In memory of Sonia Clare Biseker
In memory of Tessa Watts of Nympsfield
In memory of
 the Kennard and Gunn families
In memory of the late Christopher Rookes
In memory of
 the late Sir George and Lady Farmer
In memory of Timothy and Jacqui Reilly.
 Share our joy.
In memory of Tom and Josephine Steel
In memory of Tony Hyde,
 Lover of the Arts
In recognition of David Brierley's splendid
 service with the Royal Shakespeare
 Company 1961-1996 (General Manager
 1968-1996)
Ira Aldridge
Irene Worth - donor Donald Seawell
J B Bland
J C Trewin
J F M Bland
Jackie Howell Purnell 1943 -
James and Katie Bradshaw
James Arthur Laws
James Marsters
Jan Norton
Jane Drabble and Bill Nemtin
Jane Grove
Jane Lapotaire
Jane Snowden
Janet Suzman
Janice and Robert Atkin
Jeanie Holland
Jennifer Hilary. Incomparable Actress
Jenny Abramsky and Alasdair Liddell
Jenny Bowes
Jill and Ken Taylor
Joan Mountford, Hannah, Ben and Eleanor
Joan Newstead
Joan, Frank, Lucy and Jill Carruthers
Joanne Taylor
John and Anita Weeks
John and Betty Ratcliffe
John and Catherine, Ruth
 and Christopher Caulkin
John and Jan Hornby
John and Judith Theakston
 "The play's the thing"
John and Mary Mott
John and Peggy Souter
John and Suzanne Goddard
John B Shaw, Professor of English
 1955-1989, Hiram College USA
John Caird

John Crisp and Ian Kirk
John Drew
John Fenwick
John Hencher and John Cupper
John J. Studzinski CBE
John Lucken
John Philip Kemble
John Purkis
Jonathan and Paula Bate
Jonathan, Christopher and David Tilley
 in memory of Pamela
Joseph Jefferson Holland
Joy and Dennis Nisbet
Joyce Alice Wilkins
Joyce, George and Frederica Hauger -
 may the fun continue
Jude Hirst and Family
Judi Dench - donor The American Friends
 of the RST Inc. through the generosity
 of an anonymous donor
Judith M. E. Evans
Julia Marlowe
Julia Paton
Julian and Jenny Cazalet
Julie Byczynski and Angus Gray
K. Edmonds Gateley MBE
Katharine Hepburn
Katherine Zorzy-O'Gorman
Kathleen and Stanley Whitehouse
Kathy Rooney
Kay Barlow
Kay Pascoe for family, friends, pupils
Keith and Roy Hopwood, Penarth
Ken and Marcia Scott
Kevin Taylor
Kirsty Anson
Komisarjevsky - donor Sidney Bernstein
Laurence Edward Evans
Lawrence and Elizabeth Banks
Lawrence Barrett
Lee and Melinda Varian
Lela Macbean
Lewis Waller
Linda and Peter Chadwick
 of Beggarly Broom
Linford Cazenove. Our Inspiration
Little Miss Lucy Wood, Grandma Goodfox
 and Grandpa Ed
Liz, Alan and Edie Pollock
Lord Alexander of Weedon QC, 1936-2005
Lorna Flint 1918-2008 whose love of
 Shakespeare inspired so many
Luke and David Warner
Luke Richardson
Lydia and Manfred Gorvy
Lyn McKay
M.L.C. Floreat Salopia
Madge Titheradge
Marcia Whitaker

Margaret (O'Hara) Howell 1897 - 1972
Margaret Leighton - donor Michael Codron
Margaret Smith and Jenny Brown
Margery and Harry Cox
Marian and Leonard Mathews
Marian and Roger Pringle
Marianne Williamson
Mark and Jackie Rowlands
Mark and Sandy Foster
Mark Leipacher
Mary and John Holmes, Calverley, Leeds
Mary Anderson
Mary Hunt and Charles King-Smith
Mary Weston
Masashi and Yoko Sakai
Maureen and Jeff Locke
Maureen Joan Lewis
Maureen Woodhead "A Lass Unparalled'd"
Maurice and Jean
Michael and Ann Rowen
Michael and Anne Heseltine
Michael and Jane Lyons
Michael and Jill Clapham
Michael and Sheila O'Sullivan and family
Michael and Susan Clasper
Michael Boyd and Vikki Heywood
Michael Horden - donor E R Bosley
Michael Southworth Miners
Michel Saint-Denis - donor Sidney Bernstein
Michael Weston and his family
Mick and Chris Beddows
Miles, Denise, Kate and David Tandy
Min and David
Miriam Stoppard and Chris Hogg
Miriam Valentin Seva. San Diego, California
Monica Bickerstaff
Monique Aublanc and Patricia Boden
Morag and Archie Shearlaw
Mr John and Dame Janet Gaymer
Mr. Douglas Bollinger
Mr. James Bollinger
Mrs and Mrs Charles Flower
Mrs Mary Morgan Taylor
Neil Benson RSC board member
   2001-2007 for that privilege
Nicholas Bancroft 1943-2007
Nick and Victoria Jones
Nigel and Rhona Empson
Nightingale Family
Norma Gilbert
Oliver Clark
Orson and Torin Cox
Our Theatre, Your Seat sponsored by
   Katie Newbon
Our wonderful parents -
   Fred and Jackie Gibbs - from us all
Pam and Eric Farlie
Pam and Peter Jordan
Pam and Tony Stevens

Pat Donovan donated by Stratford
   Amateur Operatic Society
Patricia Allison
Patricia and Kerry Milan
Patricia Rigby
Patricia Whitehead M.B.E.
Patrick Wymark - donor Ben Shepherd
Paul Ammann
Paul and Oonagh Hodges
Paul Scofield - donor H.M. Tennant Ltd
Paula and Hope Owen
Penelope Carnwath
Penny and Robert Freedman
Peter and Brenda Bignold
Peter and Jill Parker
Peter and Joanna Studdert
Peter and Katie Gray
Peter and Sue Davis
Peter Brook - donor The Edgar Lee
   Foundation
Peter Hall - donor Lord Birkett,
   Harold Pinter
Peter, Katy and Verity Aitken
Philip Holland
Philip and Sally Le Brocq and family, Jersey
Phillips Exeter Academy U.S.A.
Phyllis and Ray Smith
"Pray you sit by us, and tell's a tale"
   Vivien Heffernan and her son John
Priscilla Mares
Professor Paul Cartledge
Qeiva Grant
R.S.C. Hon. Assoc. Actor Richard Pasco C.B.E.
Rachel Borland
Rachel Kempson - donor Lex Service
   Group Ltd
Ralph and Bill Smith.
   Patrons for over 60 years.
Ray and Eileen Dunn
Rebecca and Daniel Hearne
Rebecca Greenwald
Remembering Gwen Williams who in her
   time played many parts
Remembering Robert Twigg -
   "The play's the thing"
Remembering Wyn Luntley
   'love all, trust a few, wrong none'
Richard and Judith Cheney
Richard and Patricia Burbidge
Richard Burbage
Richard J. Balfour
Richard L. Hay
   Oregon Shakespeare Festival USA
Richard Wilson
Richard Wilson
Rita Hannah
Robert and Carole Seward
Robert and Christine Clarke
Robert O. and Carolyn J. Perry

Robin Geoffrey Fickus
Robyn Durie
Rodney and Gail Baker-Bates
Roger and Jean Grenville-Jones
Roger P T Duckworth
   "The play's the thing"
Ros Haigh
Rosie Keep
Roz Farmer
RSC Friends
Russ and Linda Carr
Ruth and Robin Pinsent
Ruth Spencer
Sallie Purkis
Sally-Ann Fowler
Sam and Paul Jones
Samuel Phelps
Samuel Waterhouse
Sara Crystal
Sara Harrity and Jeffery Samuelson
Sarah Rachael Alford 21st Birthday
   29th November 2008
Sarah Siddons
Shakespeare's Dogs
Shakespeare's Horses
Shawen Alannah Day
Sheila and David Suchet
Shirin Irani and Darius Mirza
Simon and Nicky Salomé-Bentley
Simon Inch
Sir Alec Guiness - donor The American
   Friends of the RST inc. through the
   generosity of Winifred Raab-Weber
   in loving memory of her father
   William H Raab
Sir Derek Higgs 1944-2008
Sir Laurence Olivier
Sir Lewis Casson - donor The John Lewis
   Partnership
Sir Michael Redgrave -
   donor Paul Elliott and Bernard Jay
Sir Ralph Richardson
Sir Ronald and Lady Cohen
Sir Trevor and Lady Chinn
Sir Whitworth Wallis -
   donor Lt. Col. L Stokes-Roberts
Sophie Service
St Bernard's School
Susie Sainsbury
T C Kemp
Ted Garratt - 'The rest is silence'
Tegwen Roberts
Tessa Sidey
The Boris Karloff Charitable Foundation
The Gentilli Charitable Trust
The Hobhouse Family
The John Thaw Foundation
The Limoges Trust
The Mackintosh Foundation

The Oakley Charitable Trust
The Pidem Fund
The Protherough Family
The Shakespeare Institute,
   in memory of all our students
The Studdert-Kennedy Family
The Towers Family, Lindale, Cumbria
The Webber Family
Thomas Wright
Tilly Faust
Tim and Theresa Lloyd
Tim Pigott-Smith and Pamela Miles
Tim Sayer and Kate Wolstenholme
Timothy M Baker
To celebrate the joy of friendship
   and Shakespeare
To celebrate the life of
   Sheila Sibson-Turnbull
To mark Pat Goldsmith's 80th birthday
Tony Church. Actor. 1930-2008.
   He loved this place
Tony, Diana, Tom and Lucy Hill
Tracy Irish and Dom Giles
Trevor Nunn
Trevor R. Griffiths
Valerie Thompson
Veronica Lafferty
Victoria Riskin and David W Rintels
Viv Phillips and Friends
Vivien Leigh - donor Mrs H Bewlay,
   Mrs M Macnair, Mrs R Antrobus
Waley-Cohen Family
Walter and Jennifer Barbour
Walter Hines Page
"Well met by moonlight" MO and JL
Wellesley College
Wendy Craig
Wendy Elizabeth Ribeyrol
Wendy Roy Tim Bex Andy Sal Rob Davies
William and Joan Strang
William Charles Macready
With happy memories: Eve, Charles,
   Elizabeth and Nicholas Dee
With thanks to Mick Hughes for his
   46 years service to the RSC
With thanks: Ginnie and her Redston/
   Ross-Smith girls
Yehudi Menuhin - donor J C Williamson
   Theatres Ltd. Australasia

Picture Credits

Simon Annand/© Royal Shakespeare Company: 3. Lucy Barriball/© Royal Shakespeare Company: 20l, 58l, 80, 108tc, 109br. © Bennetts Associates: 26bl, 54, 60, 62-63, 64bc, 65, 67, 69bc, 70c, 83-84, 89-90, 92. © Charcoalblue: 26tr, 30, 56, 82. Joe Cocks/© Shakespeare Birthplace Trust: 22. © Peter Cook: Endpapers, 52, 68r, 69, 117, 119r, 120, 122-131. Malcolm Davies/© Shakespeare Birthplace Trust: 11tr. Herbert Felton for The Architectural Review: 33. Manuel Harlan/© Royal Shakespeare Company: 59bl. Hayes Davidson: 88. Stewart Hemley/© Royal Shakespeare Company: vi, 1-2, 4, 5br, 8a, 8c, 21, 24-25, 26br, 27-29, 34, 35tc, 36-37, 39br, 40l, 41, 43, 50br, 51, 53br, 57, 59br, 61, 66, 71, 76-78, 79r, 81, 85-86, 92l, 93, 94-99, 104-107, 108l, 109tc, 109bc, 110-116, 118l, 121, 125. Denis Jones/Evening Standard/Rex Features: 14tc. Ellie Kurttz/© Royal Shakespeare Company: 5l, 42, 49, 58tr, 59tl, 79l. Angus McBean/© Royal Shakespeare Company: 10. Tom Pilston: 53tl. Gina Print/© Royal Shakespeare Company: 87, 118r, 119l. FC Rickett: 64tl. © Ian Ritchie Architects: 39tc, 39br, 40l. © Royal Shakespeare Company: 13, 16br, 18, 20r, 23, 68l, 79. CP Satyajit: 38. Stratford-upon-Avon Herald: 14bc, 16tc. Flip Tanner: 55. Simon Wilding/© Royal Shakespeare Company: 48, 91. Reg Wilson/ © Royal Shakespeare Company: 11tc, 11bc.

Written by David Ward
Managing Editor Kevin Wright
Copy Editor Sally Brambles
Image research by Lucy Barriball
Design Consultant Andy Williams
Print Consultant Gina Print

Thanks to Jane Ellis, Anna McNeil, Lucien Riviere, David Howells, Michelle Morton and Flip Tanner.

Design by The Drawing Room
www.drawingroom.uk.com

Printed and bound by Hill Shorter Limited, West Bromwich

Printed on GF Smith Colorplan Bright Red/Pristine White duplex (cover), Naturalis Absolute White Smooth (text)